T0074203

The Impact of Fibre Connectivity
on SMEs

Andy Phippen • Hazel Lacohée

The Impact of Fibre Connectivity on SMEs

Benefits and Business Opportunities

Andy Phippen
School of Management
Plymouth, United Kingdom

Hazel Lacohée
BT Technology Service & Operations
London, United Kingdom

ISBN 978-3-319-47553-0   ISBN 978-3-319-47554-7 (eBook)
DOI 10.1007/978-3-319-47554-7

Library of Congress Control Number: 2016954027

Cover illustration: Pattern adapted from an Indian cotton print produced in the 19th century

Printed on acid-free paper

This Palgrave Macmillan imprint is published by Springer Nature
The registered company is Springer International Publishing AG
The registered company address is: Gewerbestrasse 11, 6330 Cham, Switzerland

CONTENTS

List of Tables

CHAPTER 1

Introduction

Abstract Connectivity is an essential part of business operations for the vast majority of organisations. This can be particularly true for rural businesses, who suffer when competing with their urban counterparts due to lack of transport infrastructure or peripheral location. Arguably, improved connectivity has a more significant impact upon their business performance than organisations in urban settings. The Superfast Cornwall project provided the opportunity to explore the impact of vastly improved connectivity upon businesses in one of the most remote locations in the UK – Cornwall. The project was a three-phase longitudinal study engaging in detailed qualitative work with local businesses to measure a broad range of impacts.

Keywords Fibre broadband · Qualitative research · Rural business · Rural SMEs · Business regeneration

The book reports on research conducted on a three-phase longitudinal study of rural small/medium enterprises (SMEs) experience of fibre connectivity, through the exploration of the experiences of the Superfast Cornwall Project (Superfast Cornwall 2016). Superfast Cornwall was a £132 million programme to bring fibre connectivity to Cornwall and the Isles of Scilly and was funded by the European Union's Regional Development Fund (ERDF programme), BT (BT 2016) and Cornwall Council (Cornwall Council 2016a), and managed by Cornwall Development Company (CDC 2016).

© The Author(s) 2017   1
A. Phippen, H. Lacohée, *The Impact of Fibre Connectivity on SMEs*,
DOI 10.1007/978-3-319-47554-7_1

The Superfast Cornwall programme started in September 2010, and ran until April 2015 with the goal of making Cornwall one of the best connected rural economies in the world, placing fibre at the heart of this transformation. Cornwall has qualified for ERDF funding because it is officially one of the poorest regions of Europe, having experienced a decline in traditional industries like fishing and mining. For example, Cornwall used to be home to the world's biggest tin mining industry, a vital component of the UK economy that helped power the British industrial revolution. However, in combination with the decline in Cornwall's fishing industry, the region has suffered from the demise of the tin mining industry (Thrift and Williams 2014) resulting in the region becoming one of the poorest in England.

The project had the potential to provide extensive economic, social and infrastructure outcomes for Cornwall and in essence, Superfast Cornwall is a case study in transforming a rural European region with fibre broadband as a key enabling infrastructure. In terms of comparison with the UK more generally, according to Cornwall Council, based on the UK Office for National Statistics, the greatest differences in business profile are that Cornwall has more agriculture and accommodation/food industry businesses and less information and communications technology, and is professional, scientific and technical than other areas in the UK (Cornwall Council 2013, Cornwall Council 2016b).

While the majority of impact studies into Internet connectivity are quantitative in nature (UK Government 2013), the approach in this study was qualitative in nature, in order to understand beyond simple quantification of impacts to study more long-term issues such as business change, job creation, innovation and process evolution. We report concerns uncovering and driving the benefits of connectivity for SMEs to help them achieve their ambitions for growth and while the focus of the data from this study is Cornish SMEs, the findings are relevant to all rural areas of Europe and further afield where improved connectivity is proposed as a regenerative technology to improve business performance and competitiveness.

There were three phases of research through the project. Phase 1 was a baseline study of SMEs' work practices prior to the introduction of fibre broadband to understand problems they had with existing provision and to gauge expectations and aspirations and drivers and barriers to take-up of fibre connectivity. Phase 2, conducted after the introduction of fibre connectivity, concerns SMEs who had been using fibre for 6–12 months and considers how this has met SME aspirations and expectations and captures drivers for adoption, business benefits and perceived economic, social and environmental impacts. The research also looks at how business can be conducted differently with greater connectivity and considers the kind of innovations that arise as a result. Phase 3 focused on longer-term users who have had access to fibre for 18 months to understand whether the findings of Phase 2 have endured, and how nascent and novel innovations, collaborations and different ways of working have developed with longer experience of use and the impact this has on conducting business in a rural location.

Our aim was to address a key challenge – the requirement for detailed work to optimise the benefits of connectivity to SMEs because a key element of the programme is to assist businesses to exploit the technology in order to secure the desired economic impact. Cornwall has a small but growing economy with high levels of self-employment (Cornwall Council 2013). Most of our sample was comprised of microbusinesses and this is typical of Cornwall and of the UK more generally; UK Government statistics for 2015 (UK Government 2015) show that there are 5.2 million businesses in the UK and 96 % (5.0 million) are microbusinesses employing 0–9 people in the UK, of these 75 % have no employees and 2.9 million operate from home (UK Government 2014). The growth in microbusinesses is thought to be a long-term trend and the contribution of micro firms to the economy is huge, hence this justifies a strong focus on this sector.

The home-based business sector is a valuable asset to the rural economy and yet there are few studies that elucidate the realities of operating a rural home-based business, or the issues and problems they face, hence our research helps to address that gap. Small businesses have been disproportionally represented in rural areas in the UK and elsewhere, but as advances and innovations in information communications technology (ICT) grow and are combined with access to a fibre-based broadband network, microbusinesses are starting to dominate the business landscape.

The structure of this text follows the timeline of the project closely. Initially, the introductory chapter will explore connectivity from a policy perspective – focusing mainly on the UK- and EU-related policy (Broadband Delivery UK (BDUK), Digital Agenda for Europe, etc.). This exploration enables us to place the Cornwall project in its broad academic and policy context prior to its in-depth exploration. We will argue and evidence that most impact studies, particularly around business regeneration and technology, will focus on economic and environmental impacts with some key quantitative metrics (such as increased revenue, carbon consumption and job creation) and as a result will miss rich qualitative data that can inform policy at an international scale in terms of fibre broadband diffusion, take-up and impact far beyond these simply measures and regardless of the location of study.

The chapter continues by establishing literature related to the adoption of innovations and how this might help inform the research approach within the project. In particular, models such as Diffusion of Innovations and the Technology Acceptance Model and its relevance to the take-up of connectivity services are explored.

The chapter concludes by defining the methodological approach in more detail, presenting a structure driven from an overall research aim to gauge the impact of fibre connectivity for SMEs in the successful and effective running of businesses in Cornwall. A number of measures were defined at the outset of the research drawing on previous literature around technology adoption, particularly associated with broadband technologies:

- Drivers for fibre broadband adoption;
- Aspirations and expectations regarding fibre connectivity;
- Speed and efficiency benefits of fibre connectivity;
- Economic benefits of fibre connectivity;
- Social benefits of fibre connectivity;
- Environmental impact of fibre connectivity;
- Business impact and ability to work differently;
- Future aspirations;
- Connectivity options;
- SME issues and concerns.

In the first chapter presenting research findings, Chap. 3 considered aspiration and ambition prior to the adoption of new technology, considering the impact of connectivity to businesses up to the start of the Superfast Cornwall project, and their expectations and aspirations of improved connectivity. In exploring the move from dial up to regular broadband services, the data showed a number of key findings:

- Broadband had served businesses well and changed the way they function but slow speeds impact when and how business is conducted and SMEs have to adapt their working practices to accommodate this.

- The initial excitement of moving from dial-up speeds to ADSL speeds soon become a business expectation, rather than benefit, and business practice "filled" the additional capacity afforded by the fast connection speeds.
- Access to the Internet is a fundamental part of business life in Cornwall, expectations of fibre connectivity are high and the majority of businesses are not happy with their current broadband provision.
- Reliability is a key issue with regular broadband and could be sufficiently frustrating to hamper day-to-day business practice as well as growth.
- While policy perspectives may look holistically at broadband adoption, it was clear that expectation differed depending on what broadband speed businesses could currently achieve. We are not starting from a level playing field with all businesses. Bearing in mind that infrastructure in Cornwall was not comprehensive, some businesses at the end of a copper line on a 0.5 megabits per second (Mbps) connection will be delighted with a shift to 10 Mbps. However, someone currently on 8 Mbps will be less impressed by this change.

We uncovered a number of expectations for the improved capacity anticipated from fibre broadband, such as working faster and more effectively; videoconferencing; reducing the need to travel; improved upload and download speeds; job creation and business expansion; opportunity to create new businesses; increased autonomy; making tasks easier to accomplish; less need to adapt business practices to accommodate slow speeds; reversing the shift from offline to online; ability to work from home; ability to remain located in the region; creating a level playing field; ability to connect more people and devices; increased opportunities for collaboration, and the ability to take advantage of Cloud services.

This set of expectations provided another layer to add to our evaluative framework when evaluating the impact of fibre broadband as the roll-out progressed across the county.

However, while in general expectation was positive, the initial baselining research also raised some interesting potential barriers, not through technology but through business expectation and the roll of interpersonal communication in adoption. Two specific issues drove this exploration, namely:

- Service provider's reputation is something that is currently hampering positivity towards the project. Many participants who had encountered poor service with ADSL did not believe that service providers were capable of delivering the project and there was an "expectation to fail".

- The perceived lack of accurate, *available*, information is being filled by those who are generally ill informed and drawing conclusions based on poor knowledge foundations.

Given the importance of social and communication channels for the successful adoption of new innovations defined within the literature, the concerns and adoption barriers raised by this negative expectation was significant at the start of the project and potentially had a severe negative impact upon the project.

However, in Chap. 4, where adoption had taken place we could explore far more positive attitudes. In this chapter, we explore the early impacts of fibre connectivity on businesses which presented an interesting challenge in drawing out what those benefits might be. It was interesting to note that those who had moved to adopt were extremely positive about it, but in general could not articulate that into effective business benefits. "Better", in a lot of cases, just meant doing the same things with a faster connection. However, once explored in more depth, it became clearer that adoption was swift and embedded extremely quickly into organisations, which was probably why it took some effort to get them to reflect on value. A number of key benefits could be identified:

- Rural businesses who traditionally suffered from remoteness from extended markets discovered fibre connectivity offered new-found access to global markets that is continuing to promote business growth and enables SMEs to create new revenue streams.
- We found an increased use of Voice Over IP (VOIP) conferencing (such as Skype) where participants described how this facility had significantly reduced telephony costs, reduced the need to travel and increased opportunities for collaboration by providing a new, rather than simply an improved way of working. We saw an increasing use of VOIP application across different sectors to communicate with clients.
- We found increasing evidence of participants accessing a broader customer base as a result of fibre connectivity. Better connectivity is providing SMEs with greater confidence, enabling them to broaden their customer base within the UK and further afield and this is supporting business growth in the region.

- In facilitating the use of Cloud services, fibre connectivity offers SMEs the opportunity to revolutionise the way they work and compete far more effectively with their larger rivals. Cloud services offer SMEs the opportunity to reduce their IT expenditure and this provides flexibility and frees up funds that can be directed towards other aspects of the business.
- Fibre connectivity is enabling SMEs to remain located in Cornwall, protecting existing jobs and is providing the infrastructure that helps overcome the region's peripheral location. There was evidence of job creation but employment patterns are changing with increased collaboration on short-term contracts both locally and farther afield.

It was also interesting to note that the negativity expressed opinions of baseline focus groups which went unchallenged were countered from early adaptors who could present positive experience to challenge those who had an "it's never going to happen" attitude. Hands-on experience heavily influenced the very positive views expressed regarding attitudes towards fibre connectivity and helped to overcome any apprehension SMEs may have felt initially. Having experienced fibre connectivity, the value it provides has become deeply embedded in SMEs daily work practices and processes and promotes efficiency, productivity and competitiveness.

What became clear was that the longer the organisation had fibre broadband, the more effectively they would use it, and the greater the opportunity for new practice and innovations. We refer to this as the "virtuous circle of connectivity" – a chain of interdependent benefits of fibre broadband that have become so important to SMEs that they have become far more reliant on that connectivity than they were on regular broadband. SMEs have achieved not just an improved way of working, but different ways of working. As SME reliance on those benefits grows, that increases and reinforces their value, new dependencies are forged and a new set of values and benefits emerges that are used to even greater effect.

In Chap. 5, longer-term impacts were studied through the exploration of Phase 3 of the project. Phase 3 analysis not only extended our exploration of the impact of fibre broadband on rural businesses but also explored the potential issues that arise through its availability and adoption. One issue that arose the more embedded the technology became was that this is not simply a case of technology deployment and optimisation of business benefits. Upskilling of the workforce is still an issue, and for some SMEs, the belief that they know enough to operate effectively is still hampering any upskilling potential and in turn this hinders growth. A major reason for this lack of insight is that participants are not aware of what it is that they do not know.

In addition, while deployment was wide ranging across the region it was clear that connectivity was still not as inclusive as businesses believed it could be – they were critical of fibre broadband roll-out and lack of availability and poor connectivity in what they perceived to be key geographical areas such as town high streets and business parks. Again this is driven by increasing business dependence on connectivity.

However, in studying longer-term impacts we did see increased diversity of benefits and raised aspirations once the potential of fibre connectivity had been experienced by participants. When asked about their future aspirations, participants' requirements are wide and varied but speed and reliability are still at the top of the list; all participants said they need a guaranteed fast, consistent and reliable service and one that provides excellent customer service. The technology also high-lighted flaws in other business essential infrastructure. For example, businesses aspired to being able to work wirelessly and via mobile services, especially when working from home (a perceived benefit of improved connectivity) but several had experienced technological difficulties. Ostensibly, Wi-Fi, smart phones and Skype mean that SMEs can work wherever they choose but with poor mobile signals in many parts of Cornwall and thick granite walls in many local properties hampering wireless connectivity, these opportunities are not as widely available as they might be.

Cloud services emerged as a major disruptive force as a result of fibre connectivity. Few participants had used Cloud services prior to the intro-duction of fibre because of slow connectivity but many had considered this ability as potentially transformative for business, hence it was a strong driver for adoption. Cloud technology offers a fundamentally different way for SMEs to harness computational power, storage capacity and services and is boosting innovation as a result.

We had also begun to see changes in employment patterns although these were less clear than what might be anticipated from business growth. While there was little evidence of redundancy as a result of improved technology, there was more evidence of short-term collaboration than long-term employment. SMEs were collaborating with others on short-term contracts rather than employing them full time.

Environmental factors, which were explored in detail in the research against an often proposed hypothesis that technology will be appealing to companies if it reduced their carbon footprint, were also discussed. However, we found SMEs are more driven by economic factors than environmental or sustainability factors, although when explored there were knock on sustainability benefits such as reduced travel to work, travel out of county, reduced printing, etc. However, the picture is not a clear-cut as some might believe, with some evidence simply of carbon shifting rather than reduction.

In bringing together all of the research findings, Chap. 6 brings together the strands of research, exploring "lessons learned" which have implications for business research and policymakers, as well as other regions deploying such technologies.

What is clear is that the path to adoption is not as straightforward as one might envisage and benefits are more wide ranging that purely faster connectivity. Our research showed that fibre broadband can make substantial contributions to the conditions required for inward investment in Cornwall. Different ways of working made possible with fibre connectivity result in the development of new products and services, business diversification and enhancement, new revenue streams, a broader customer base, greater control and improved competitiveness.

Technological innovation has led to more services and more people owning more devices that all require bandwidth. The ability to connect more people and multiple devices through fibre broadband without compromising quality of service or speed of operation is a valuable asset to business.

One of the other more interesting findings was that dualistic thinking that separates work and home as distinct categories for broadband provision is outdated and inappropriate. Advances in ICT and access to fibre connectivity have given rise to a large market of home-based microbusinesses of growing economic significance that have been largely ignored to date. Microbusinesses operating from home have long been thought of and referred to as "invisible businesses" because (erroneously) they were not thought to make a significant contribution to the economy. As a result, until recently, they have been largely ignored by government, policymakers and service providers alike as of little consequence. Legislation and regulation have been designed for a world in which the workplace and the home are separate and this needs to be challenged.

Access to fibre broadband acts as a motivator to upgrade IT equipment to make the most of connectivity but there is still a knowledge and skills gap in the SME community in understanding how fibre is delivered and what any limitations might be. Rather than offering training opportunities that are unlikely to be taken up by SMEs who do not recognise their need, a business mentoring scheme is likely to be more effective.

We conclude by recommending that policymakers and technology providers look beyond the "build it and they will use it" model of connectivity roll-out. What is clear from our research is that motivations for adoption come from a number of factors; it is not simply a case of making things faster. Business needs to understand what the benefits of adoption will be through effective information channels, and they also need a knowledge and skills base to fully deploy and exploit the potential of new technologies. What is clear from our research is the improved connectivity can have a significant impact upon SMEs, but those benefits are realised over a long period of time and short-term policy successes are not substitute for real impact.

REFERENCES

BT. (2016). BT website. http://www.bt.com [Accessed August 2016].

CDC. (2016). Cornwall development company website. http://www.cornwalldevelopmentcompany.co.uk [Accessed August 2016].

Cornwall Council. (2013). Cornwall's economy at a glance. https://www.cornwall.gov.uk/media/3624042/Cornwalls-economy-at-a-glance.pdf. [Accessed July 2016].

Cornwall Council. (2016a). Cornwall council website. http://www.cornwall.gov.uk [Accessed August 2016].

Cornwall Council. (2016b). Cornwall's economy at a glance. https://www.cornwall.gov.uk/media/3624042/Cornwalls-economy-at-a-glance.pdf [Accessed August 2016].

Superfast Cornwall. (2016). Superfast Cornwall website. http://www.superfastcornwall.org/ [Accessed August 2016].

Thrift, N., & Williams, P. (2014). *Class and space (RLE social theory): The making of urban society.* London: Routledge.

UK Government (2013). Spending Round 2015/16 - full details of funding for DCMS bodies published. https://www.gov.uk/government/news/spending-round-201516-full-details-of-funding-for-dcms-bodies-published [Accessed July 2016].

UK Government. (2014). Backing for home-based business boom. https://www.gov.uk/government/news/backing-for-home-based-business-boom [Accessed July 2016].

UK Government. (2015). Business population estimates for the UK and regions 2015. https://www.gov.uk/government/uploads/system/uploads/attachment_data/file/467443/bpe_2015_statistical_release.pdf [Accessed July 2016].

CHAPTER 2

Defining the Research Context

Abstract The Superfast Cornwall project exists within a broader policy context that seeks to drive improvements in broadband connectivity, particularly fibre broadband, across countries – driven by government to encourage investment in infrastructure by private sector telecommunications companies. Superfast Cornwall, specifically, can be related to both European (Digital Agenda for Europe) and UK (Broadband Delivery for the UK) policies. In understanding how take-up of such projects may become successful, we can draw from established technology adoption theories to consider factors beyond technical availability. Informed by policy and literature, the research context defines a detailed three-phase approach looking at those considering adoption, early impact, and long-term benefits, considering a broad range of success factors beyond simple economic benefits to consider things such as social value, environmental impact and barriers to adoption.

Keywords Fibre broadband · Qualitative research · Technological adoption · Diffusion of innovations · Technology acceptance model

The Superfast Broadband project in Cornwall, UK, has its root in a wider policy context of business regeneration and development through improved technology infrastructure and connectivity, with

© The Author(s) 2017
A. Phippen, H. Lacohée, *The Impact of Fibre Connectivity on SMEs*,
DOI 10.1007/978-3-319-47554-7_2

11

this policy driven from both a UK and European perspective. Over the last few years, there have been a number of lobbying and policy initiatives that aimed to promote wider investment in broadband infrastructure.

2.1 Policy Context

Nesta (2009) raised concerns that the UK was lagging behind the developing world's drive to invest in digital infrastructure to facilitate business regeneration and growth. They claimed that the barrier in the UK was mainly to the high cost of Fibre to the Cabinet (FTTC) and Fibre to the Premise (FTTP) provision (Nesta 2009). Nesta called for major investment in the UK to replace the current telecommunications infrastructure, which relied upon a copper cable background which, therefore, would also have contention and capacity issues, with fibre optic.

In 2010, the European Commission launched the "Digital Agenda for Europe" (European Commission 2010a), one of seven flagship initiatives that form part of the Europe 2020 Strategy. The main objective of this initiative was to "chart a course to maximise the social and economic potential of ICT".

The Commission had recognised that information communications technologies (ICTs) had a significant impact upon the nation states, with 20 % of the EU's productivity growth comes directly from the efficiencies afforded by ICT, and another 30 % comes from ICT investments. However, it also recognised that the EU was not effectively benefiting from the potential of digital developments. In particular, when considering investment in high-speed Internet access (i.e. fibre optic-based connectivity), European investment was poor compared to competitors like South Korea and Japan.

The focus of the Commission's aim for "maximisation of the social and economic benefits of ICT" was to increase the availability, across the EU of 30 megabits per second (Mbps)+ connections, they also declared an aspiration to develop a greater capacity for faster (sometimes referred to as "ultra-fast") connectivity of over 100 Mbps. Overall, the aim was for the whole of the EU to be able to access speeds above 30 Mbps and 50 % to be able to use connections of over 100 Mbps.

In addition to underlying infrastructure, the agenda consider the following broader issues related to the effective exploitation of improved connectivity:

The key components of the agenda include measures to address:

- A perceived lack of digital literacy and skills;
- Insufficient research and innovation efforts;
- Addressing interoperability issues through the definition of a "single digital market" to address the fragmentation of digital economic activity (particularly eInvoicing and electronic payments) along national boundaries.

In 2012, 2 years after the Digital Agenda had been published, the Commission produced a review (European Commission 2012) to consider developments to date and also to set out additional areas of activity in order to further reap the benefits from improved infrastructure. These included:

- The improvement of public sector innovation and interoperation through information exchange. "A Digital Agenda for Europe" identified weaknesses in standard-setting, public procurement and coordination between public authorities as preventing digital services and devices used by Europeans working together as they should;
- The implementation of an eHealth Action Plan which aims to develop integrated care solutions across regions reaching 4 million EU citizens by 2015;
- Regaining world leadership of network services through addressing the concerns raised by market uncertainties, and to provide incentives for private investment in both fixed and mobile broadband infrastructure;
- A European Cloud Computing Strategy in order to coordinate the exploitation of the potential of Cloud-based services, which are realised through more effective connectivity. The strategy proposed the development of pan-European Cloud platforms to connect national public Cloud initiatives; and
- The launch of a grand coalition on digital skills and jobs.

In part as a response to the Digital Agenda for Europe, but also in response to lobbying pieces such as the Nesta report, BT, the organisation who provide the majority of telecommunications in the UK, announced in 2010 (IT Pro 2010) that they would invest £2.5 billion to deliver fibre optic broadband to 66 % of the population by 2015. This was part of a major investment to upgrade the national infrastructure.

In the same year, the UK Government's department for Business Innovation and Skills (BIS), and the Department for Culture, Media and Sport (DCMS), aimed to enhance the European agenda by setting out ambition targets to enable the UK to have the best fibre optic infrastructure in the Europe by 2015 (UK Government 2010). To achieve this, the UK Government, through Broadband Delivery UK (BDUK), allocated £530 million to the roll-out of high-speed broadband in rural communities and £150 million for an Urban Broadband Fund to create "super-connected cities".

Overall, investment in superfast infrastructure in the UK, as a result of a combination of national Government, local Government and EU money, reached over £1.7 billion, with an aim to extend coverage to 95 % of premises by the end of 2017. In February 2015, DCMS published figures (UK Government 2015) to indicate that the project had extended superfast broadband to more than 2 million homes and businesses and was on course to meet the 2017 target.

Since the publication of the baseline report the government has released new details about its Rural Community Broadband Fund, this fund is designed to complement BDUK and includes a £10 million BDUK investment and a further £10 million from the Rural Development Programme for England. The fund will be available to projects to support those 10 % of areas which will not receive superfast broadband under BDUK. The fund is open to applicants from charities, community groups and social enterprises throughout England, except Cornwall and the Isles of Scilly. In 2011, the government set aside £100 million for an "Urban Broadband Fund" to create 10 "super-connected" cities, across the UK. A further £50 million of funding was announced in 2012 for an additional 12 cities. The money was to fund "ultrafast" broadband of 80–100 Mbps in addition to increased public wireless Internet access. In addition, £150 million is being provided through the Mobile Infrastructure Project to improve mobile coverage in areas with poor or no coverage. More recently, the government announced a £250 million investment as part of the Spending Review

2013 to ensure that 95 % of homes and businesses have access to superfast broadband by 2017 (UK Government 2013). This figure was expected to be match funded locally and was targeted at those areas that are hardest to reach.

However, in Cornwall and the Isles of Scilly, one of the most rural and remote areas of the UK, funding for the ICT infrastructure has not come from BDUK, but the EU Convergence Project (Convergence Cornwall 2007) and its private sector investment partner – BT. The Next Generation Broadband Infrastructure project, known as Superfast Cornwall, was funded by a £78.5 million investment by BT and a contribution of £53.5 million from the European Regional Development Fund (ERDF) which resulted in a total project value of £132 million, making it the largest single Convergence investment within that portfolio of projects.

The project ran 4 years after a previous long-term ERDF investment in broadband between 2001 and 2007. The "Actnow" project was the UK's first public–private broadband partnership, brought broadband coverage from almost 0 to 99 % as well as brought an estimated £80 million to the economy of Cornwall and the Isles of Scilly (European Commission 2010b). The Actnow project was extremely successful in moving a lot of Cornish businesses from dial up (56 Kbps or below) to far higher broadband speeds, in some cases as much as 8 Mbps. However, due to the reliance upon the copper cable infrastructure in the county, many businesses and household still had far less optimal connection speeds. While broad impact measures were taken, there was little in-depth research that looked beyond pure economic impact upon businesses and certainly little qualitative analysis of adoption, maturation and long-term value to business.

The evaluation of the Actnow programme found that the Internet is critical for 87 % of businesses within Cornwall (Marketing Means 2010). However, the research found that the vast majority of businesses simply used their connectivity for basic IT functions, such as e-mail, searching for information and buying goods and services. Those who had achieved transformative business operations as a result of improved connectivity were certainly in the minority with only 39 % of businesses using the Internet for funds transfers and payments and 32 % using it for social networks (although given the time period over which Actnow ran, social media had far less ubiquity than it does now, and it would certainly not have been considered a business essential).

However, despite significant EU and UK investment in Actnow, the Cornish economy was still identified as requiring "catalytic and transformational interventions" if it were to move towards being a knowledge-based economy (Convergence Cornwall 2007). Given the remoteness of the county and the lack of large-scale transport infrastructure a number of traditional business sectors struggle in the county, however, the coastal geography and low population density meant it was appealing for small business in areas such as digital and ICT if appropriate, sustainable broadband infrastructure could be provided, therefore making a potentially thriving area for knowledge-based businesses where transport infrastructure is less important than connectivity. At the outset of the superfast broadband (SFBB) project, investment in digital infrastructure in particular was identified as an important mechanism through which the negative effect of the lack of viability of transport-dependent sectors could be mitigated. The roll-out of superfast broadband on this scale was therefore considered to support the economic priorities for the county.

Compared with BDUK investments in other parts of the country, the Convergence funded Superfast Cornwall project was unique for three reasons:

- Investment: The largest single European investment in superfast broadband;
- Scale: The world's largest rural area covered by superfast broadband; and
- Penetration: The largest number of FTTP covered in the UK.

The region of Cornwall in the UK presents both challenges and opportunities when considering the impact of fibre broadband technology on a region given its remoteness, lack of high-speed transport infrastructure and fractured nature of the business community (the vast majority of businesses in Cornwall are Small/Medium Enterprises (SMEs) and micro-businesses). Therefore, it could be argued that a region such as Cornwall has more to benefit from the roll-out of fibre broadband compared to a more urban area when connectivity options would already be in place.

2.2   RESEARCH APPROACH

Therefore, if we consider the SFBB project in Cornwall, we can see that is does not exist in isolation, but with a very broad policy context for business competitiveness and development across the whole of the EU.

The impact of SFBB upon Cornish businesses is not merely of interest within the region – it represents the opportunity to study the long-term adoption and impact of vastly improved Internet connectivity within a region, to explore what worked, what did not and what were the barriers to success. We hoped that, as a result of the in depth exploration of the impact of SFBB upon SMEs in the Cornwall, we would be able to pass on lessons learned and recommendations to future initiatives and also articulate the importance of holistic strategies when considering technology adoption upon this scale (and arguably with such a strong social factor). Technology adoption is a complex research domain, and it is not simply the case of "build it and they will adopt".

Rogers' "The Diffusion of Innovations" (2003), arguably the most thoroughly established and researched attempt to understand how innovations are adopted by organisations, proposes that there are a number of factors that influence and individual's choices with regard to an innovation within an organisational context. While available of an innovation is important, without other factors, its adoption will be slow or may be none existent. Alongside the innovation itself, Rogers defined three other key factors:

- Communication channels;
- Social system;
- Time.

The famous S curve of adoption showed that different types of organisations adopt technology at different rates – innovators will jump upon new innovations quickly, followed by early adopters, early majority, the late majority, then finally those defined by Rogers as "laggards". While the "majority" will adopt a technology as a result of a critical mass of others using the technology, without the innovators and early adopters, this critical mass may never be achieved. In general, Rogers defined larger organisations as being more conservative in their adoption and small, more agile, companies being more like to adopt early. Therefore, for a technology such as SFBB, given the very high proportion of small and microbusinesses in Cornwall, we might propose that there is a high likelihood, based upon Diffusion of Innovation theory, that the adoption of SFBB will be successful. However, if we consider the other factors defined in the theory, there are also challenges. Straub (2009) suggests that communication channels and the social system are key components of the theory, highlighting the important of interaction among peers are part of the adoption process. Therefore, it was important to consider sources of information afforded by potential adopters of SFBB, and how they developed their knowledge of the innovation. This is explored in far more detail in the following chapter, but it is worth noting that the importance of information sources and information sharing are underpinned so strongly in the theory.

In more recent times, Davis's Technology Acceptance Model (TAM) (Davis 1989) has become the more widely accepted model for innovations adoption. Developed in 1986, with the purpose of examining individuals and the choices they make to accept or reject a particular innovation within information technology (Straub 2009). In addressing some of the failings in Diffusion of Innovations, such as the complexity in being able to "prove" factors that caused innovation adoption within complex human systems. Conversely, TAM aims to track how external variables can affect internal beliefs, with both Perceived Usefulness and Perceived Ease of Use being the two most important factors of the model. The crux of this is the *perceived* usefulness and ease of use – while the perception may not be borne out in reality, if potential adopters can be convinced that the technology is both useful and ease to use, they are more likely to adopt.

However, while both of these long-established theories are useful in guiding what we may explore with SMEs on their adoption journeys related to SFBB, we also need to acknowledge that both of these theories were developed in a time when communication was far less connected, and, arguable, the influence of social factors is now more important than ever. Therefore, when developing the research aims for this piece of research, we were careful to look at the social and influencing factors in a lot of detail.

2.3   DEVELOPING THE RESEARCH APPROACH

The aim of the research was to gauge the likelihood of the adoption of SFBB among business and subsequently the impact of fibre connectivity for SMEs in the successful and effective running of businesses in Cornwall. Overall, a number of measures were defined at the outset of the research drawing on previous literature around technology adoption, particularly associated with broadband technologies:

- Drivers for fibre broadband adoption;
- Aspirations and expectations regarding fibre connectivity;
- Speed and efficiency benefits of fibre connectivity;
- Economic benefits of fibre connectivity;
- Social benefits of fibre connectivity;
- Environmental impact of fibre connectivity;
- Business impact and ability to work differently;
- Future aspirations;
- Connectivity options;
- SME issues and concerns.

Overall research was conducted in total with 20 focus groups of between 10 and 15 businesses held between April 2011 and 2015, in total comprise 400 hours of discussion around the aspirations for and adoption of SFBB, and its short- and long-term impact. In addition, follow-up interviews and in-depth interviews with particularly interesting cases were conducted comprising another 20 hours of data collection.

Through the course of the research, over 200 businesses participated in the analysis. While there was phased research with specific outcomes and set times, such as aspiration and expectation, short-term impact and longer-term impact the focus throughout was on SMEs and microbusinesses and over the course of the project the types of businesses in the sample included (Table 2.1):

Our sample was comprised of microbusinesses (0–9 employees) and this is typical of Cornwall and of the UK, more generally. Government statistics for 2015 (UK Government 2015) show that there are 5.2 million businesses in the UK and 96 % (5.0 million) are microbusinesses employing 0–9 people in the UK, of these 75 % have no employees and 2.9 million operate from home. However, actual numbers of microbusinesses are likely to be much higher because hundreds of thousands fall below government measures, that is, businesses that are not a limited company and fall below the VAT registration threshold (have an annual turnover of less than £79,000) are not counted in national statistics as a trading company. These sole proprietors are more likely to be home based than office based and many are online only businesses that operate on domestic contracts.

The growth in microbusinesses is thought to be a long-term trend and the contribution of micro firms to the economy is huge, hence this justifies

Table 2.1   Business types and number at focus groups

Type of business	Number of companies
IT management	20
Retail	22
Tourism and hospitality	34
Creative design, digital and media	25
Architecture	5
Accountancy	6
Management and business services	25
Education and training	10
Plumbing	2
Financial services	5
Funeral directors	1
Construction	8
Disaster recovery services	1
Motor trade	5
Publishing	2
Agriculture	12
Utilities	5
Healthcare	8
Transport	4

a strong focus on this sector. The home-based business sector is a valuable asset to the rural economy and yet there are few studies that elucidate the realities of operating a rural home-based business or the issues and problems they face, hence this study helps to address that gap. Small businesses have been disproportionally represented in rural areas in the UK and elsewhere but as advances and innovations in information communications technology (ICT) grow and are combined with access to a fibre-based broadband network, microbusinesses are starting to dominate the business landscape.

Focus groups were professionally facilitated based on agreed discussion guides (see Appendix), recorded and fully transcribed. Field notes and observations were also recorded through focus groups to contribute further to mood, opinions and session dynamics.

These overarching themes were decomposed into a phased research design which incorporated three periods of data collection, in order to achieve a longitudinal research path overall. While all of these phases contributed to the overall research aims, they also had a specific focus, described further.

2.4   Phase 1 – Early Adopters and Those Wishing to Adopt

2.4.1   Phase 1 – Research Aims

The aim of this phase was to create a baseline study of SMEs behaviour and attitudes prior to the introduction of SFBB in Cornwall. We aim to provide an understanding of the following:

- Current experiences and problems with existing broadband provision;
- Visibility and availability of information about SFBB;
- Aspirations and expectations of SFBB;
- Attitudes towards SFBB and perceived barriers to take-up;
- Perceived drivers and benefits for take-up;
- Perceived social and environmental impact.

The key objectives of the study are for learning from the Cornwall SFBB study to be fed into other similar bids (e.g. Northern Ireland), for Cornwall to learn from other rural deployments, and for the Cornwall deployment to inform best practice in other geographies.

2.4.2   Sample

Research was conducted with five focus groups between April and July 2011. Representatives of local SMEs were recruited, with the majority coming from north and west Cornwall with over 74 businesses participating in this research.

2.5   Phase 2 – Those Who Had SFBB for up to 6 Months

2.5.1   Phase 2 – Research Aims

The aim of this phase was to gauge the impact of SFBB for SMEs in the successful and effective running of businesses in Cornwall:

- Drivers for SFBB adoption;
- Aspirations and expectations regarding SFBB;
- Speed and efficiency benefits of SFBB;
- Economic benefits of SFBB;

- Social benefits of SFBB;
- Environmental impact of SFBB;
- Business impact and ability to work differently;
- Future aspirations;
- Connectivity options;
- SME issues and concerns.

The key objective of the study was for learning from the Cornwall SFBB study to be fed back into the second half of the Superfast Cornwall Programme so that changes can be made to ensure the best outcomes for the programme. Additional objectives were to inform other BDUK and NGA bids, for Cornwall to learn from other rural deployments, and for the Cornwall deployment to inform best practice in other geographies.

2.5.2   Sample

Research was conducted with four focus groups held between July 2012 and April 2013. Participants were drawn from a randomly selected sample of businesses in areas that had been SFBB enabled for 12 months plus. Representatives from the local SME community who had signed up for and used SFBB for between 6 and 12 months were recruited from 72 businesses across a range of sectors.

2.6   PHASE 3 – LONG-TERM ADOPTION AND IMPACT (18 MONTHS USE OF SFBB)

2.6.1   Phase 3 – Aims

The overall aim of this phase was to consider and understand the long-term impacts of the adoption of SFBB upon business operation, development and innovation. As such, it aimed to explore:

- Whether SFBB has continued to meet SMEs aspirations and expectations over time;
- Whether speed and efficiency benefits of SFBB have endured;
- Enduring business impacts and ability to work differently as a result of access to SFBB;
- SME innovation as a result of SFBB;

- SME's ability to maximise SFBB benefits;
- SME's future aspirations and future proofing;
- Connectivity options and FTTP;
- SME issues and concerns.

A key objective of the study was for learning from Phase 3 to be fed back into the final phase of the Superfast Cornwall Programme so that, in combination with Phases 1 and 2, we can provide a longitudinal view of the impact and value of fibre connectivity for SMEs in the region. Additional objectives are to inform other BDUK and NGA bids, for Cornwall to learn from other rural deployments, and for the Cornwall deployment to inform best practice in other geographies.

2.6.2 Sample

Research was conducted with six focus groups held between March 2014 and April 2015. Participants were drawn from a randomly selected sample of businesses in areas that had been SFBB enabled for 18 months plus. Representatives from the local SME community who had signed up for and used SFBB for 18 months or more were recruited from 60 businesses across 28 sectors.

2.7 CONCLUSION

The SFBB project in Cornwall should not be viewed in isolation. It should, instead, be seen as an early pilot project (albeit one with unique private/public funding in the UK) to consider the impact of improve fibre connectivity upon business performance, development, regeneration and innovation. While there are unique characteristics within the project (such as the funding model, but also the nature of Cornwall's business composition, the remote location and low population density, the lack of traditional industry or large corporate organisations) the project fits very much within the broader context and aims of both BDUK and EU policy around deploying fibre optic-based Internet connectivity in order to give companies within the regions a competitive edge.

However, while much evaluation of the impact of technology upon business is driven by quantitative measures which provide easy and quotable statistics for policymakers to quote to illustrate successes, lead from theory around technology adoption and acceptance, we have taken a deliberately broad and inclusive view upon what "successful" looks like and how it is achieved.

In the next three chapters of this text, we present the findings from the three phases of this research, to illustrate the broad range of findings and factors that have impacted upon the successful adoption and acceptance of SFBB by SMEs in Cornwall. It illustrates very clearly that availability is not the only factor that results in the adoption of technology, and, particularly where organisations have had previously bad experiences with similar technology, the need for information and knowledge building alongside the technological innovation. However, it also shows the positive impact of adoption, and how truly transformative new technology can be once embraced and understood by organisations. In particular, we define a theory of the *virtuous circle of connectivity*, which highlights that benefits have a cumulative effect, and while short-term impacts may be interesting, the truly revolutionary tends to take time to take hold.

References

Convergence Cornwall. (2007). ERDF convergence. http://www.erdfconvergence.org.uk [Accessed July 2016].

Davis, F. D. (1989). Perceived usefulness, perceived ease of use, and user acceptance of information technology. *MIS Quarterly, 13*(3), 319–340.

European Commission. (2010a). Digital agenda for Europe (English version). http://eur-lex.europa.eu/legal-content/EN/TXT/PDF/?uri=CELEX:52010DC0245R(01)&from=EN [Accessed July 2016].

European Commission. (2010b). ACTNOW: Transforming Cornish business through broadband communications. http://ec.europa.eu/regional_policy/EN/projects/best-practices/ALL/1467/download [Accessed July 2016].

European Commission. (2012). Digital agenda for Europe scoreboard 2012. https://ec.europa.eu/digital-single-market/sites/digital-agenda/files/KKAH12001ENN-PDFWEB_1.pdf [Accessed July 2016].

IT Pro. (2010). BT adds £1 billion to fibre rollout to cover two-thirds of UK. http://www.itpro.co.uk/623254/bt-adds-1-billion-to-fibre-rollout-to-cover-two-thirds-of-uk [Accessed July 2016].

Marketing Means. (December 2010). Cornwall development company next generation broadband business survey: Autumn 2010. Results.

NESTA. (2009). Getting up to speed: Making super-fast broadband a reality. https://www.nesta.org.uk/sites/default/files/getting-up-to-speed-report.pdf [Accessed July 2016].

Rogers, E. (2003). *The diffusion of innovations*. (5th ed). New York: The Free Press.

Straub, E. (2009). Understanding technology adoption: Theory and future directions for informal learning. *Review of Educational Research*, 79(2), 625–649.

UK Government. (2010). 2010 to 2015 government policy: Broadband investment. https://www.gov.uk/government/publications/2010-to-2015-government-policy-broadband-investment/2010-to-2015-government-policy-broadband-investment [Accessed July 2016].

UK Government. (2013). Spending Round 2015/16 – full details of funding for DCMS bodies published. https://www.gov.uk/government/news/spending-round-201516-full-details-of-funding-for-dcms-bodies-published [Accessed July 2016].

UK Government. (2015). Business population estimates for the UK and regions 2015. https://www.gov.uk/government/uploads/system/uploads/attachment_data/file/467443/bpe_2015_statistical_release.pdf [Accessed July 2016].

CHAPTER 3

Moving Up the Information Superhighway

Abstract In Phase 1 of the research, the focus of enquiry was around the impact of "traditional", ADSL broadband upon rural businesses, the problems organisations faced in its adoption and the aspirations for connectivity within their businesses. Problems reported included slow broadband speed, and the contention ratios associated with ADSL. Aspirations for fibre broadband included an expectation of a more reliable service (reliability is considered as important as speed for most organisations) and greater access to third online services. Businesses also expressed many beliefs around why superfast broadband (SBFF) would not work, based on a lot of the time on simply untruths and rumour, although this exploration did highlight the need for accurate, available information when considering technology adoption.

Keywords Fibre connectivity · SMEs · Rural business · Barriers · ADSL · Information

In this chapter, exploring results from the research, we consider the impact of connectivity to businesses up to the start of the Superfast Cornwall project, and their expectations and aspirations of improved connectivity. Bearing in mind that, even with regular broadband, some companies may have been moving from a connectivity of 0.5 megabits per second (Mbps), even the introduction of basic superfast broadband (SBFF) at around 10 Mbps made a considerable difference to their Internet access. This early baselining work

© The Author(s) 2017
A. Phippen, H. Lacohée, *The Impact of Fibre Connectivity on SMEs,*
DOI 10.1007/978-3-319-47554-7_3

considered expectation and assumptions from the new service, and was conducted very early in the project. Therefore, the majority of the finding is related to pre-SFBB provision and the issues of a small/medium enterprise (SME) operating with unreliable or slow connectivity.

In conducting this exploration, we uncovered a number of expectations for the improved capacity anticipated from fibre broadband, such as working faster and more effectively; videoconferencing; reducing the need to travel; improved upload and download speeds; job creation and business expansion; opportunity to create new businesses; increased autonomy; making tasks easier to accomplish; less need to adapt business practices to accommodate slow speeds; reversing the shift from offline to online; ability to work from home; ability to remain located in the region; creating a level playing field; ability to connect more people and devices; increased opportunities for collaboration, and the ability to take advantage of Cloud services.

However, while in general expectation was positive, the initial baselining research also raised some interesting potential barriers, not through technology but through business expectation and the roll of interpersonal communication in adoption.

3.1   Moving on from ADSL

When broadband was first introduced in Cornwall and the Isles of Scilly, it was warmly greeted by SMEs in the region as providing them with an opportunity to compete on a level playing field by providing access to the technological infrastructure that exists elsewhere in the UK and abroad. This was felt to be particularly important in Cornwall because the county has a poor road and rail infrastructure; there are only two major road links between Cornwall and the rest of Britain. Many SMEs felt that access to a technological communications infrastructure via broadband could diminish some of the disadvantages of the county's peripheral location, and it was seen as a major step change for small businesses. However, less than a decade later, SMEs in the region are experiencing problems with their broadband provision that impact their ability to conduct business efficiently and effectively, leading some to consider relocating elsewhere:

> If we can't get Superfast Broadband in order to expand to a nationwide company we have to move out... either I've got to close the company or move, relocate out of Cornwall and I don't want to do that because I love it down here. Business Services

Fast, reliable broadband is essential to running a business productively, and work patterns and business practice are dictated by useable broadband. Cornwall's rural location and dispersed population means that many SMEs experience slow broadband connections because they live some distance from the exchange that serves their premises. Broadband is delivered over copper wires and the signal degrades with distance, delivering ever decreasing speeds depending on the distance of the business from the exchange.

3.2   Problems Associated with Slow Broadband Speed

We asked SMEs about their current experiences and identified several problems with their existing provision that impact negatively on their ability to conduct business. All groups reported a high degree of dissatisfaction with current broadband speeds and reliability of service and claimed that this changed the way that business is conducted:

> We are communicating with several factories and sending designs and quite large files across, half an hour later it is still sending one email. Graphic Design

Some participants reported losing connectivity altogether and this had a serious impact on productivity and revenue generation and in some cases resulting in lost orders and reputational damage:

> If my systems go down my money stops coming in. Retail

> I have lost orders through BT because I couldn't send or receive any; I have lost a lot of orders. I need fast upload and download because I send information and my orders through and I have to receive the electronic delivery notes back through again and I am losing them with BT. Retail

We found evidence of a peculiar perception amongst some SMEs – a belief that broadband speeds in Cornwall are slower than other parts of the country,[1] even though connection speeds register as the same. This was the first hint that perhaps conjecture had more of a part to play in the influence of the adoption approach:

> The Internet in Cornwall is just slower, even if you have the same connection speed. My grandfather lives in Manchester, he has got an 8 meg connection,

and I have an 8 meg connection, but anything on his computer that you click on, it's on the screen immediately, I was in the university in Manchester and it was the same case. Then as soon as I come back down to Cornwall, I have the same speed theoretically, and I have used other peoples in other houses, but the Internet is just slower here. Management Consultanc

3.2.1   Contention Ratio Problems

Participants reported feeling constrained by the speed of their current broadband connection, and described the impact of contention ratio problems on the ways in which they had to adapt their working patterns to accommodate slow speeds at certain times of day. It was not uncommon for SMEs to report working very unsocial hours, often late at night or very early in the morning to avoid periods of heavy Internet traffic. One problematic peak period, observed by many businesses we spoke to, was when children get home from school and go online:

> The worst time is four o'clock when the kids come home from school, pretty much. Half past three, four o'clock, until probably nine o'clock at night. It will just crawl. It's when you start working on bigger projects, where you have to have these big files flying around the country it becomes a problem. Business Services

> I go on early in the morning, because everyone seems to think late at night is good so everyone goes on then. Graphic Design

Many SMEs work long hours including evenings and weekends and these periods were also problematic due to increased consumer Internet traffic, and this was particularly difficult when participants were dealing with customers and suppliers in different time zones:

> My clients are always on, effectively. If they are not in this country then they are in another, so yes, I do get to sleep sometimes, but your business model – effectively, because I work from home, it is very easy for me to fashion my business around when my clients need servicing. Often I'm working overnight, and if I've got a critical set of uploads to do, then I'll definitely be working overnight because I know the traffic levels are a damn sight less. Creative Media

It was interesting to note that SMEs lay a proportion of the blame for contention ratio problems on content providers such as the British

Broadcasting Corporation (BBC) whom they claim are inadvertently degrading business infrastructure. The tension arises during busy periods when children come home from school and start using the Internet or at weekends when it is used for entertainment purposes when people are consuming bandwidth through their use of iPlayer, downloading music and films, etc.:

> The other thing is avoiding weekends, Saturdays and Sundays, which actually are working days for me. Again, I get crucified by the iPlayers, people doing downloads, films or whatever. I think that the whole situation has got to be addressed on the Internet because the BBC is pumping out so much content now, and they are not taking any responsibility whatsoever for the way that they are degrading the business infrastructure.

Participants thought that content providers should be made aware of, and take more responsibility for the impact consumer consumption of their services has on SME productivity, which was an interesting reflection on the difference between business and consumer expectation, something that arose frequently throughout our research.

It was likely that some, though by no means all, of the problem with contention ratio issues is due to SMEs adopting consumer rather than business products. Given the size of a lot of the businesses with whom we spoke, it is no surprise that they were opting for a consumer broadband product, particularly those who were running a business from home and some SMEs were aware that this could cause difficulties:

> If I understand it correctly, the contention ratio on a business line is a lot lower than on a domestic line. So, for example, you will share a business line with 20 other users, maximum, whereas on a private line, you share it with 50 others. So, purely by mathematics, if your maximum outbound speed is X, you will only get one fiftieth of X, as a bare minimum. It is on a different contention level. Tourism

3.2.2   Adaptation to Accommodate Slow Broadband Speeds

SMEs described having to adapt their work practices to accommodate slow broadband speeds and whilst this was deemed necessary, it was not acceptable. Slow speeds were particularly significant when large volumes of data had to be moved and in these cases participants had no option but to take alternative measures that involved shifting from working online, back to physical means of moving large files by post or courier:

> If I'm sending a book to print for publishing, each one of those is probably about 7 or 8 Mbps that will go four or five drafts. Each one of those I really would like to go a damn sight faster than it goes at the moment. The database uploads are just vast and they sit there, they'll run for hours and you are on complete tenterhooks. And if you are on a deadline, and you've got to get the data shifted, it is almost, do you stick it on DVD and have it couriered? Publisher

> You adapt round it. If you've got to shift vast amounts of data, you shove it on a drive and £90 later a courier has got it in London for you. Architect

Several participants reported regularly using couriers to move data. Adapting behaviour was not limited to sending large files however; it also applied to backups and restores when optimal time periods had to be chosen and these were usually outside of normal working hours:

> Basically it is database loads for me. That's backups and restores. It is the restores that are the issue. I usually try and bend my way around the network so that the data is being shifted from a point where you can get a decent speed. IT Management

Slow speeds also had an impact on SMEs' ability to expand their business and we found instances where participants sought alternative solutions, for example, using compression to shift large files, and the introduction of a second broadband line to share traffic:

> I'm involved in animation and motion graphics and we are trying to get into the London market. And obviously to do that effectively we'd have to send data up and down the country, so we're looking into compression as well as broadband speeds, as two solutions basically. Digital Media

However, it was viewed by most that SFBB and it is likely that it would address many contention ratio issues and slow speed problems that concern SME's currently. Speed of broadband connection was clearly having an impact on what SMEs can and cannot achieve and many had to seek workarounds as a result. Broadband connectivity was vital to SMEs but current provision is delivering only limited benefits.

3.2.3   *Upload versus Download*

Most broadband packages are sold on the basis of download speed but upload speeds have become increasingly significant in running a business. Invariably, participants told us that upload speeds were as important as download speeds; without good upload bandwidth necessary business processes can hinder day-to-day activities. Issues concerning upload speed deficiencies always arose early in discussion which indicates that this is a major concern for SMEs across sectors; it is not confined to those that are traditionally bandwidth hungry such as media and design companies:

> My biggest grievance with BT is the upload speed compared to the download speed; it's just a joke really in comparison. If you are trying to send something and it takes you ten times as long as it does to download that particular item, it's just ridiculous. Uploading and downloading should be the same speed. Digital Media

With their current broadband provision the disparity between upload and download speeds was causing real problems for many SMEs in terms of efficiency, information being delivered in a timely fashion and business competitiveness:

> I download and upload to my supplier, I also do the same with the shops and when I was with BT I was losing that speed so my shops were selling products under priced because they hadn't received the right information and it's very important for me. Retail

> If I'm working on the distribution I have only got to download it once but I'll need to upload that 1000 times and that's a 700 meg pot, try doing that on 400 k upload you'd be there until the end of your days. IT Services

Our SMEs told us that upload speeds are "crucial" and "absolutely vital" and that at the time of the research they fall well below what is acceptable:

> I think I'm shifting around about 10 Gb of data a month, download and upload. But within that, it is probably a 10–1 or 9–1 download to upload. Anybody who is in the design industry, basically, if you need to shift designs around then you are talking about multiple versions, and needing to get them from A to B as quickly as possible. And if you are sending, then that is the real issue for you. Digital Media

> We had a situation today where we needed to respond to a very important tender, and it was something like 35 to 40 Gb of data that had to go, and we had to start that process this morning in order that we could get it all in before the deadline at five o'clock today. That's working our broadband, running at 1 Mbps outbound, consistently in Bodmin. So it took a long while to do. Business Services

The ways that our SME population use their broadband connection was evolving and what they need from their service providers was changing too. Our discussion revealed that participants who formerly pulled in and downloaded more information than they pushed out were finding that they now need to upload increasing volumes of data. Ideally what SMEs would have liked was a symmetrical connection that would ensure the fast flow of data both in and out, rather than faster speeds per se. Sending and sharing files is a common practice across all business sectors; it is no longer primarily the domain of those engaged in the design or media business. Collaborative working was also increasing and this was likely to compound the problem for SMEs and place increasing demands on bandwidth as the need to share documents quickly and efficiently grows. The same was true of flexible and remote working where smooth integration with a dispersed workforce is paramount.

3.3   ASPIRATIONS AND EXPECTATIONS REGARDING SFBB

The value of SFBB to SMEs depends on how it is used and the changes it enables in any given context. SFBB needs to offer more than incremental value over broadband, it must deliver advantages and enable services and applications that are dependent on significant amounts of bandwidth. We asked participants what this might look like from the SME perspective as part of an ideal SFBB experience.

3.3.1   *Reliability and Consistency of Service*

Many of the problems SMEs currently experience with existing broadband connectivity are related to slow speeds, we might then expect faster speeds to be top of the list of participants' aspirations. This was not the case, the value of SFBB for SMEs was not correlated with speed alone, what is important is a reliable and consistent service:

We are all saying we would like it better . . . and then faster. What does better look like? More consistent. Consistency is far more important to me. Business Service

The most valued aspect of SFBB was that it can provide an overall improvement in quality of service and this has an all-round beneficial effect on SME's ability to conduct their business in the most efficient manner. The bottom line is that SMEs want better, faster, more reliable broadband but "better" is a priority.

3.4   VALUE-ADD SERVICES

Participants talked to us about the kind of value-added service they would like and highlighted the ability to solve technical problems quickly. Fast-tracking technical problems were very important because when systems are down, businesses are losing money. SMEs needed a fast response and personal service was a strong selling point. We found that participants were prepared to pay a premium for support packages that provide a personal, dedicated contact to get the level of service they require, even if they feel it is expensive:

At work and at home my ISP is ridiculously expensive but it works . . . they run their own data centres, it isn't rented in some dark site. I pay £40 per month for that and I am quite happy paying for it, I have that level of service, I can call up Richard on the end of the phone, I need this done, 5 minutes later it's done. IT Services

SMEs clearly appreciated and valued the personal element, dealing with a single point of contact with whom they have built a trusted relationship, who understands their technical set-up and the problems they encounter, and can respond immediately:

Smaller, more personal contact is definitely good. Businesses are run on trust; if you give your word on something you have got your name on it. I know some ISPs are huge but it needs to think about this at a trust level, if someone is going to deliver a product that you are paying for you want to be able to speak to whoever it is and go "I am not getting the service, fix it." Accountancy

3.4.1   Guaranteed Minimum Speeds

One difficulty that SMEs reported in choosing a supplier to deliver required broadband speeds is that Internet Service Providers (ISPs) advertise speeds "up to" rather than speeds that can actually be delivered to particular premises and this was deeply unpopular. Participants voiced a strong desire for guaranteed minimum speeds rather than speeds "up to" and felt that this would be more honest. We found a sense of "not getting what I paid for" amongst participants when "up to" broadband speeds were not achievable:

> I want something that works at my speed. Architect

> When broadband first came in there were all sorts of companies saying "you will get up to" and it rapidly became that everyone knew you were never going to get anything like that. And I assume that I'm not the only person that was totally annoyed about this. I do think that it's time for somebody to say, "we guarantee that you will get," you know. Tourism

Broadband speeds that are advertised as "up to" are very misleading, it sets up unrealistic expectations and leaves participants feeling confused and cheated when they do not deliver the maximum:

> I'm not getting what I'm paying for...I'm still not getting what they promised; it should be a sliding scale. 40 meg is £40 and if you're giving me 20 meg I'll pay you £20, that seems fair. Retail

In the current economic climate, access to cutting edge technologies that help SMEs to perform more efficiently, at an optimal level, have never been more important. SMEs in the region are making efforts to sustain innovation but need the flexibility to react to external pressures and opportunities and SFBB can provide them with an important competitive edge.

3.5   ATTITUDES AND PERCEIVED BARRIERS TO SFBB

The move from dial up to ADSL was seen as a major step change for SMEs but they were some convinced of the value of SFBB:

> It's a bit like in the early days of electricity. You used to have one light or one appliance and that was it. Now of course we have them all over the place, we

need electricity everywhere, it's an integral part of our life and broadband is now an integral part of our business life and our personal lives. Tourism

Everything I have seen so far...Superfast Broadband is a technology looking for an application. IT Services

One thing that was articulated very strongly from our attendees was that they are very reliant on the Internet access for fundamental business operations, and broadband had enabled their businesses to effectively communicate and carry out information-processing functions in a manner where they are now reliant upon it. The change in the use of ICTs moving from dial up to broadband has been both life and business changing. However, what is equally clear is they are unsure about whether SFBB will result in a similar change in working practices – whether it is evolution rather than revolution. What was interesting was that these attitudes were not developed as a result of using the technology, but overall opinions developed either as a result of using existing broadband and discussion with others:

Before you had to boot up your PC and then you had to press a few buttons and then you had to actually dial it up and you couldn't make a phone call and now you're online all the time, my router is permanently on, my laptop is there and well, you are connected. I don't think you're going to get that kind of leap and I think also if you are sending and receiving some emails you aren't going to notice any difference. It's only when you are sending data or pulling data down, sending big images or you are actually surfing a badly written website. Business Services

It's faster than it is, but not faster enough! IT Services

It terms of what sort of speeds would be desirable, many were talking about 100 Mbps+:

If I could get a gigabyte I'd be laughing. Digital Media

One thing that emerged very quickly from our discussions was that the asymmetric nature of SFBB was an issue for some technology businesses. While they valued the increased download speed, the nature of the sector, particularly in moving to offsite backup and data centres, upload speed is becoming increasingly important to them (and will continue to be so) and this could not be provided by SFBB – even though they were not aware that the increase in upload speed might be sufficient for their needs:

> It's a halfway house. This is really a halfway house. I'm a bit disappointed in it to be honest. My business relies on clients being able to upload data to us. Business Services
>
> The average multi track file is about 5 gigabytes now and that's a lot of data to move around. I could actually drive to London quicker than I can send it. Digital Media

What became apparent from a number of discussions at these groups was that there are a significant number of high-tech micro- and small businesses in Cornwall who were operating in spite of, rather than because of, the current infrastructure. In one particular instance, an attendee felt concerned enough to be considering relocating his business *away* from Cornwall:

> I was very disappointed to find out that once the Convergence funding for making Cornwall Superfast gradually took the emphasis off FTTP it seems a watered down solution to keep the home users happy. I need lease lines, I think there's a few people around here I've identified need lease lines, but the ISP says, no we're not rolling that out even though you are a St Agnes telephone number which wasn't what we were told and that's being taken up. It's also trying to get an order in, it's a stop gap, it's not what Cornwall needs if we are going to make the most of Convergence and really challenge the rest of the country. I don't want to move my business back to London but if things don't happen soon.... Business Services

A lot of discussion centred on the target market for SFBB. While the belief was it was being marketed as a business product, many of the businesses we spoke to felt it was better suited, mainly as a result of its asymmetric nature, to the consumer marketplace, where download/upload ratios are far more heavily centred on the download:

> I think Superfast Broadband is brilliant for the home consumer but today we are not consumers. Everyone sitting around this table has either got their own business or representing a large corporate or medium sized corporate and for the corporate environment we need much more, and you can't give it to us or if you do, it's the cost. Business Services

Superfast is great for the home consumer who is going to dip in and out and find that they can download their videos when they want to much faster than they can at the moment. Digital Media

What also arose from these discussions were the age old road/traffic analogies. Participants discussed that simply providing "more road" did not necessarily mean faster transport:

You put an extra lane on the motorway, and what happens is quite quickly that extra lane fills up. Now, I understand fibre optics is a lot more than putting just one more lane on the system, but one suspects that what will happen is that you will get more and more and more traffic and eventually, we may be looking at the same situation. I think we will be. It is a question of time scale. Tourism

It's a maximum of 40 mb for business but what's the contention ratio? What's it going to be like at half past five when the kids come home and start doing their homework? That's a real problem down here. Business Services

We also discussed at length that SFBB is not the complete solution. While fast broadband access is important to business, in order to move to a twenty-first-century technology infrastructure, it is only one piece of the puzzle. Again, there were assumptions about the technology without much evidence that this was based upon a deep-seated knowledge of the technology:

The other thing I'm thinking about is, we've talked about a lot and it keeps getting mentioned, is saturation of it, it will eventually come over 80% of Cornwall by 2014. There are two things with it that concern me, one, it's the same problem that you have with all broadband is the difference between upload and download is still huge and also, unless the ISPs and the infrastructure behind it is going to cope with the significant increase in traffic that you'll get with the amount of increase in bandwidth, will it, once it gets saturated, suffer from the same problems that normal broadband does now where you get peaks and troughs in the day where it will plummet because you've got everybody downloading massive great files? That's the other concern I have with it. It's great now, but in 5 years time it could be just as bad as normal broadband. Business Services

It will, it will degrade especially when you get things like the pay per view video services being rolled out, they just suck up so much bandwidth. IT Services

Infrastructure, for example, robust and accessible data centres, is also part of the requirement for the new business infrastructure, but one thing that continually arose in these discussions was that, as previously discussed, reliability and consistency of network were as important as speed:

> There is no point in talking about all of these wonderful speeds that can be achieved, unless they are commercially backed up there is no point in businesses going for it. In addition to that as well there is a hundred and one different ways of actually skinning the IT cat because we have already mentioned that you can outsource servers to server farm. Server farms are unattended these days, big, big server farms, they are all unattended, you could easily outsource your IT infrastructure and put it on a far more reliable platform by actually going to professional data centre companies. Business Services

This above quote very clearly articulates the issues faced by businesses if they are being asked to place their businesses in the hands of other peoples' technical infrastructure – if they know what they are going to get they can plan and forecast. However, if they become reliant on a certain level of access and reliability that then degrades as a result of increased take-up, for example, their business can become vulnerable. It was very clear from our discussions that reliability is as, if not more, important as speed.

The two converging issues of SFBB as a consumer product and business need for reliable and consistent service moved our discussions on to what possible solutions there might be for this issue, that is, what might convince a business to sign up for SFBB as a viable business solution. The majority of suggestions centred on a "two-tier" service – one for business and one for consumers:

> Unless the organisations put an equivalent, or tier one infrastructure in just for business, everybody is going down the same pipe at the end of the day and more people will take it up. Businesses don't increase that quickly here but the number of households that switch onto the new facilities of faster broadband is massive. Retail

> That is going to make a difference. Also, I would want to know whether or not I'm paying for business traffic, segregated. Tourism

Transparency was a key issue that arose for those discussing service provision, particularly given their experiences previously with ADSL roll-out.

This highlighted how previous negative experiences can have a serious impact on future expectations:

> Transparency is one of the key things, ISPs needs to restore the confidence that we have lost in the last 10 years.

As discussed above, the issue of not knowing how much bandwidth you are getting is an issue for business customers. Our participants felt that ISPs should be open about the likely capacity available, rather than just maximum, or in some cases, one may suggest unrealistic expectations:

> Part of that is just having a transparency so that you see exactly the services, here is my top line, here is my bottom line and if I am somewhere in between those two lines then I am a happy customer, if it goes below I want a discount or credit on my account, if I go over because I need to then I am happy to pay more because I am needing more. IT Services

> But as a business you should be paying business rates...it should be unlimited. Business Services

3.6 Misconceptions, Paranoia and Untruths!

However, it became a point when the expectations and attitudes were driven by some fairly incredible opinions, often delivered by focus group participants as fact. While in our exploration of attitudes towards SFBB and our learning from our time with participants, we should stress that while some opinions are well formed and business knowledge is good, there was also a considerable amount of poorly formed knowledge which would, again, hamper adoption routes while having no foundation in reality:

> One of the problems that we had recently was nothing to do with Superfast Broadband, we actually had all our emails go down because of the issues with Amazon and Cloud computing and when it was hit over in America. So I would be more interested in understanding what the ISP is going to do to make sure that their servers don't go down. The hackers are going to get at the servers around the world and if we'd stayed with the really poor service provider that we were with before we swapped ISPs, we wouldn't have lost our emails. We actually lost them over the Easter weekend which was pretty disastrous for us and because of our techy guy he was able to swap

everything on the servers, but the ISP as far as I was concerned, a huge company like that and they can be brought down?. Tourism

In this quote, we have great example of how people form an opinion based on a completely inaccurate knowledge base. It would seem that this participant had lost their e-mail services as a result of an attack on their application provider. However, they are also sure that this is down to their service provider. The blame, as far as they were concerned (and this particular individual generally had a negative view of their ISP) was down to their service provider. However, all their ISP provided was a route onto the Internet, and has no control over application provision – regardless of their ISP if their application provider was attacked, there is nothing that can be done at a network level. In addition, we had another participant who believed their *intranet* access was slow as a result of their broadband connection:

> With me working at home, as soon as I try to access anything on the Council intranet, I've got to go and make a cup of tea and come back again. It's so slow it's almost unusable. Business Services

While the participants are almost contradicting their own beliefs (i.e. their connection speed is only slow when they are accessing the work intranet) they did seem to feel that their broadband speed from home to the workplace was at fault, rather than it being a problem inside the work networks.

In some cases participants almost became inciters to other members of the group, by claiming knowledge that was simply untrue:

> I come from the big bad corporate world and where you are basically basing a network on lease lines and if you have 100 meg going into the Internet you will get 100 both ways. There is absolutely no reason whatsoever why ISPs can't deploy the same technology as part of the Superfast Broadband offering to enable companies to actually achieve that kind of connectivity both ways. Business Services

We would certainly agree that "a little knowledge is a dangerous thing" in this domain. Those with some technical knowledge, or purporting to have technical knowledge, became the focus of a lot of the discussion, with other participants directing their questions away from the facilitator, and towards their new knowledge source. In these situations, we deliberately stayed away from correcting poor or inaccurate knowledge. We wished to observe the sorts of dialogue that would go on in the public domain and it was an interesting relationship to explore – those who were viewed as the technical experts certainly thrived on the attention they received and those asking the questions were very easily convinced by what they were told:

> You won't get the speeds down here because there isn't the infrastructure actually out there in the cloud in order to get the data centres down here, it is simply not there. You have to have lots and lots of fibre going out into industrial parks or wherever you want to put a data centre, you simply won't get it, no infrastructure. IT Services

This quotation was also particularly interesting to us, because it makes no sense at all! While there are lots of technical words in the statement, there is very little knowledge. It seems our participant has decided that SFBB is some kind of Cloud service, rather than an infrastructure project, and is getting confused, claiming that such will not work without fibre to the premise, which is exactly what the project is proposing!

Within our exploration of misconceptions, it is apparent that again there was a lot of mistrust in service providers and much paranoia about their business practices:

> I cannot understand why service providers should be in that state because they have got the best fibre optic kit, which we all put up with the insertion a few years ago when they had the main highways up for the whole summer from a mysterious place down at Lands End, the opposite end of the county. Someone else is obviously getting the benefit of our disruption because we are certainly not seeing it; there is no excuse for that, the kit is all there. Business Services

There were a few mentions of the FLAG Atlantic 1 connection that comes out of the sea at Porthcurno as part of the major network connection between the UK and North America. Sometimes it was described as a "secret" that conspiratorial participants shared with their colleagues. There seemed to be an assumption that because there was a large fibre optic connection that went through Cornwall, service providers should just be able to tap into this cable to provide unlimited access across the county.

There was also mistrust and concern about service providers preventing some participants from getting access to the new service, for a variety of reasons:

> We cannot get the Superfast Broadband although we are on the exchange at St Agnes, the service providers have decided not to roll it out to the farmland around where we are based. The technology is also limited on distance from the exchange and it's greatly attenuated compared with the existing broadband. Tourism

This participant (who ran a rural tourism business) was claiming knowledge of the physical properties of the various ways of providing broadband, and had the total misconception that attenuation in fibre is higher than in copper, whereas the opposite is true. However, because they used a technical term, and spoke with authority, their comment was taken up with great interest and concern by a number of participants who lived distances from their local exchanges.

We also heard concerns over security, particularly with relation to Cloud services. One particular comment stands out that encapsulates many of the issues around knowledge, particularly as it came from someone who had never used Cloud services:

> But there is a trust issue, do we trust the cloud? We have just had this with one of the gaming people, they had all of their records hacked, the Chinese have cracked all of the emails for the security guys in the US – I can't see anyone wanting to look at my records and I don't do my baking online or anything like that. Tourism

Within this single quote, we have evidence of misinformation, ignorance and fear. While sometimes we focus on skills as the driver for adoption and exploitation, we would suggest that we are not far enough down the adoption curve to consider skills needs in any great detail.

We also had a participant who did not think they would get SFBB because of the copper infrastructure and trees near their premises:

> One of the things that I would like to see is a very, very clear understanding of how ISPs are actually inter-working with each other in order to provide the service going out to the third party suppliers that ultimately depend upon the ISP to actually provide these services. You talked about Superfast Broadband being a service which is delivered by fibre to the cabinet, the issue I have is very simple, you have got to get out there and support the people on the copper in order to deliver these services, I know from first hand that because of the interworkings within ISPs, if you

have a problem, ultimately it comes down to a copper problem out there in amongst all of the trees and yet there is no proactive programme on the part of ISPs to go out and actually clear all of the trees away from the copper because of those people who are dependent on the copper in the rural areas. Tourism

Finally, we had interesting, misinformed views on how ISPs throttles traffic in busy periods, with one participant convinced that they have policies to control network access at night:

> It's the management, it's traffic shapes, the same way that ISPs traffic shape all of their connections now, which is why your connections drop at 5 pm because the ISPs have a traffic management policy which kicks in between 4 and 11 at night. I know a couple of people have told me in the last couple of days that their connections at around 8 or 9 pm plummeted where they can't actually browse through Google. Business Services

While exploring misconceptions was not one of our original aims in discussion of attitudes towards SFBB, we feel this is a crucial aspect of learning around technology adoption in social contexts. The formation of "technical gurus" in our focus groups reflects what happens in informal social settings. Without anything to challenge misconceptions, the dissemination of inaccurate information can be rapid. Unless accurate information can be readily available, and complete, the gaps and questions will be filled and answered by those who feel they are, rather than actually being, sources of authority. When coupled with the mistrust of service providers that have been endemic throughout our focus groups, such misinformation can be dangerous and potentially very harmful to the project. There was clearly an education piece to be done to explain exactly what is being delivered, why, where and to whom, how fibre works and the difference between fibre and copper.

From this exploration of our early discussion around SME expectations of connectivity and the anticipated arrival of SFBB, we see a number of key issues:

1. Connectivity is a key issue to remote businesses (of which one might argue Cornwall is entirely comprised);
2. Lack of fast, reliable connectivity can have significant business impact;

3. Reliability is as important as speed;
4. Expectations for new services (such as SFBB) are tainted by previous experiences;
5. If there is a vacuum around information of new technology, it will be filled with prejudiced or just incorrect information.

In the subsequent chapter, we move from expectation to reality, exploring the early impact of SFBB from those who adopted it as soon as it became available.

NOTE

1. This is a belief that Internet speeds are actually slower in Cornwall than elsewhere in the country, participants were of the opinion that this had nothing to do with contention problems. There was also discussion amongst participants about how speeds had been much slower since Christmas and a perception that this had something to do with SFBB installation.

CHAPTER 4

Early impact – Take-Up and the Virtuous Circle of Connectivity

Abstract Phase 2 of the research explored early adoption (less than 6 months) to consider what early gains could be understood from the adoption of fibre broadband by rural small/medium enterprises (SMEs). Organisations demonstrate clear, benefits so that the IT function become more mainstream and business process could rely upon reliable, fast connections. We propose the virtuous circle of connectivity, where increased use of connectivity results in a continuous improvement. Further benefits included better work/life balance, new ways of working and greater use of Cloud services. However, issues still arose, such as the lack of skills and knowledge to effectively exploit the potential of the technology and concerns over business reliance on connectivity that was still prone to failure.

Keywords Fibre connectivity · SMEs · Rural business · Cloud services · Skills gap · Virtuous circle of connectivity

In this chapter, we move on from considering expectations and attitudes towards a sharp increase in capacity and connectivity for small/medium enterprises (SMEs) to looking at the reality of the early impacts of fibre on businesses. It was interesting to note that those who had moved to adopt were extremely positive about it, but in general could not articulate that into effective business benefits. "Better", in a lot of cases, just meant doing the same things with a faster connection. However, once explored in more depth, it became clearer that adoption was swift and embedded extremely quickly into organisations, which was probably why it took some effort to get them to reflect on value.

It was also interesting to note that the negativity expressed in the opinions of some baseline focus groups which went unchallenged were countered from early adopters who could present positive experience. Hands-on experience heavily influenced the very positive views expressed regarding attitudes towards fibre connectivity and helped to overcome any apprehension SMEs may have felt initially.

What became clear was that the longer the organisation had fibre broadband, the more effectively they would use it, and the greater the opportunity for new practice and innovations. We refer to this as the "virtuous circle of connectivity" – a chain of interdependent benefits of fibre broadband that have become so important to SMEs that they have become far more reliant on that connectivity than they were on regular broadband. SMEs have achieved not just an improved way of working, but different ways of working. As SME reliance on those benefits grows, that increases and reinforces their value, new dependencies are forged and a new set of values and benefits emerges that are used to even greater effect.

4.1   EARLY ADOPTION AND IMPACT

This "Phase 2" research, conducted after the introduction of superfast broadband (SFBB), considers how fibre connectivity has met SME aspirations and expectations and captures drivers for adoption, business benefits and perceived economic, social and environmental impacts related to the introduction of SFBB in Cornwall. The research also looked at how business can be conducted differently with greater connectivity and considers the kind of innovations that arise as a result.

Access to fast, reliable broadband is fundamental to running a business efficiently and working patterns and business practices are dictated by effective broadband connectivity. Phase 1 of our research revealed that the majority of SMEs were unhappy with their existing broadband provision and had high expectations of fibre connectivity. Cornwall's rural location and dispersed population means that many SMEs live some distance from the exchange that serves their premises, hence many have been working with less than optimal speeds.

It should be noted that the magnitude of the transition to SFBB from regular broadband provision was not the same for all SMEs in Cornwall however; regular broadband provision across the county is variable, hence participants are entering this arena from different starting points. Like regular broadband, SFBB is retailed on an "up to" achievable speed basis hence the speeds businesses received, whilst vastly improved over regular access, still varied across participants.

4.2   DRIVERS FOR SFBB ADOPTION

Discussions began with a focus on participants' decision process in upgrading to SFBB to uncover the major drivers for adoption. Overwhelmingly, decisions were driven by issues and problems concerning regular broadband connectivity. These were dealt with in detail in Chap. 3 and are touched on only briefly here in for clarity. Other drivers include a strong desire to expand business and improve productivity, increased bandwidth potential for uploading and a desire for better reliability.

4.3   OVERCOMING THE PROBLEMS OF POOR CONNECTIVITY

Frustration with existing regular broadband provision was the major driver for choosing SFBB. The most often cited difficulties included the impact of slow speeds and lack of a reliable and consistent service on SME's ability to run their businesses efficiently and effectively:

> I think the broadband connection I have got now is fantastic, it's dropping off sometimes but compared to what I had before it is amazing. So the actual job of providing the Superfast Broadband has been great, but it's more than that, it is much more than that, it's not just the broadband it's the frustration that I had before, I mean I was at my wits end! Well, I will admit, I was in tears. Business Services

In the light of such comments, unsurprisingly participants were delighted with the greater connectivity of fibre broadband:

> When I go on and check, it says you are faster than 95 % of the UK, so I must be faster than most people now. Tourism and Hospitality

Cornwall's SMEs are very resourceful and had devised various work-arounds to address the problems they experienced associated with poor and unreliable broadband. Many of these makeshift "solutions" were far from ideal and impacted heavily on what SMEs were able to achieve, to the extent that many described themselves as being "in despair". The problems of poor connectivity and the extreme workarounds participants had to devise to combat these difficulties created a strong driver to switch to SFBB.

In the course of discussion, it was clear that SMEs were aware of and value the greatly improved connectivity of SFBB, and were appreciative of the advantage it provides to Cornwall's businesses. Many had been hampered by problems associated with slow connectivity and SFBB has helped overcome the difficulties they experienced that stood in the way of productivity and business expansion.

4.4 Increased Potential for Business Growth

Another important driver for better connectivity was SMEs desire for business growth. Participants had already started to exploit the benefits of SFBB and felt it had exceeded their expectations and although they had only had access for up to 12 months, they could already see how it offered potential for business growth:

> I want to expand my business and the broadband was going to be the limiting factor I think, it is about how many people I can communicate with. Management Consultancy

Participants were excited about the possibilities of SFBB, even if they had not yet brought their ideas to fruition:

> The exciting thing for me it has made my business model and what I plan to do completely different, I will be able to widen it to a much larger operation than I would have with a land line system because I can communicate with more and more people. Potentially my business could be ten times bigger than it is now, probably more. Accountancy

Business growth is vital in today's financial climate and several SMEs said their ability to operate at all, particularly in Cornwall, was wholly dependent on greater and more efficient connectivity. This is particularly significant in Cornwall where road, rail and air infrastructure is poor:

> There's only a very slow train from Exeter and we had to fight to keep the sleeper. Architecture

Cornwall's peripheral and rural location makes access to SFBB very important to existing SMEs and their enthusiastic take-up clearly illustrates its value. SFBB was supporting businesses in the region with strong growth ambitions and fibre connectivity also had an important role in making inward investment to the county more likely and opportunities for start-ups more appealing.

4.5   INCREASED CAPACITY

The way SMEs use the Internet for business has changed and the increased upload capability of fibre connectivity in particular was a significant driver for choosing SFBB. As can be seen from some of the discussion, there were significant increases in connectivity for some businesses:

> That's what I was after to be honest, even if I didn't have the fast download, I wanted the upload, I've gone from 720 k to about 15 megs, that is a real difference, I mean a phenomenal difference. Management Consultancy

> It was the main thing for us, the upload speed. The ISP would always guarantee a certain level of download and for us, being website designers, upload is now much faster and that's important. Media and Design

Several participants located their need for increased upload capability in innovations that have been made in applications, software and services:

> The software we use is upgraded each year and it becomes more and more complex. Our product, our drawings become bigger and bigger and bigger because they become more and more useful. We were lucky enough to be in one of the first exchanges in this area to get Superfast and we had it immediately. Accountancy

Upload speeds have become increasingly significant in running a business; the way the Cornish SME population used their broadband connection had evolved. For the majority of SMEs, upload speed was now as important as download speed and this is not just confined to those business sectors that are traditionally bandwidth hungry. SFBB meant that SMEs could easily accomplish tasks that were difficult or impossible before and this allows them to work much more effectively. The increased bandwidth capacity of SFBB means that a growing need to upload large documents, as well as download, can be accommodated with ease.

4.6   INCREASED ACCESS TO CLOUD SERVICES

Innovations in Cloud technology offer a fundamentally different way for SMEs to harness computational power, storage capacity and services, but slow connectivity has been a major barrier to access. Few participants had used Cloud services prior to the introduction of SFBB but many were keen to do so and considered this ability as transformative for business, hence it was a strong driver for adoption. In particular, the increasing need for greater bandwidth both now, and in the future, was centred on the ability and growing requirement to take full advantage of Cloud services to operate more effectively:

> It's made working with Cloud services a lot more possible, if you're using the Cloud you need it to be fast or it's a waste of time, we're using those services all the time now, there's no delays, it's very good. Publishing

Speed and convenience contribute to the power of Cloud services as a driver but information communications technology (ICT)-related operational expenditure is also a feature:

> It's just so useful, if you store everything on the Cloud and then when I am out and about with my iPad I have got access to everything that I have got on my Mac at home, so it's brilliant. Digital Services

In order to take full advantage of Cloud services, some participants said that in the future they envisaged requiring even more upload capacity and some saw a future where their work could be conducted entirely from the Cloud:

> In the future I would like to see that you don't have a hard drive on your computer you just pack it full of RAM and work off the Cloud. Architecture

Primarily, participants were using Cloud services for hosting, back-up, storage, project management, extra processing power, virtual office access whilst on the move and to save space and the expense of in-house IT implantation costs. Increased use of Cloud services is likely to have a significant economic impact, offering access to computational power, storage and resources that were previously unattainable to most SMEs in the region, either because slow connectivity hampered use or because necessary alternative ICT expenditure was prohibitive. In this context, SFBB offers the opportunity to transform business processes for SMEs by providing essential Cloud-friendly capability.

4.7   Aspirations and Expectations regarding SFBB

In this section of the discussion, we asked participants whether their experience of SFBB had met with expectations and how it compared with the move from dial-up to ADSL.

4.7.1   Experiencing SFBB

Prior to the arrival of SFBB, and before they had an opportunity to experience the improvements, advantages and opportunities it provides, participants reported having negative attitudes towards SFBB which supports what we found in Phase 1 of the research, before the introduction of SFBB:

> Back in April last year when BT implemented Superfast Broadband we were a bit negative about it as business people, we felt we were being used as guinea pigs because we felt that the system would crash. Funeral Directors

However, having experienced SFBB, SMEs were enormously positive and appreciative of the advantages fibre connectivity provided and felt it had helped them overcome many of the frustrations of previous regular broadband provision:

> It allows you to do things that you could never count on doing before. There are the eureka moments when you look at something and think, well perhaps I could do it in a different way, and you find you can do it in a different way because you have got Superfast Broadband. So you can send large files, you can communicate virtually instantly with almost anyone, so

this does change the way you work, and looking now at the way I work compared with even a year ago when I first got Superfast Broadband, I have definitely changed the way I work.

For others, the change was not as great as the move from dial-up to broadband but even so, SFBB was cited as providing more confidence in connectivity:

> I don't think Superfast is as big a step change for me. What I am doing couldn't be done on dial-up, so when broadband arrived, that's when it started, that was the big step. The step to Superfast gives a bit more confidence and saving of time but actually it's not such a big step as it was to broadband. That was the big one. Financial Services

A minority, though very satisfied with SFBB, thought the newly achievable speeds should have been delivered earlier and that regular broadband should have been more effective:

> It's my expectation of how it should work, what I felt I should have been receiving from broadband really. I am happy with what I have got at present but really, I should have had that 2 years ago, 3 years ago, with that service then. IT Management

SME views concerning how much of an impact fibre connectivity had on their business were influenced by the business sector in which they were engaged, how they used their connectivity, and how reliant they were on communication and ICT generally. Those who relied heavily on connectivity to run their business were most vociferous and enthusiastic about the capability of fibre, but even those who were less reliant were deeply appreciative of the difference it made to conducting business:

> It depends on what you're doing with the broadband as to how much of a jump it is but it's made an enormous difference to us in our design business. Creative Media and Design

Our participants enthusiastically adopted SFBB as soon as it was made available. This was not because they were early adopters however; in fact many described themselves as not very technically proficient. Instead, they signed up for SFBB largely as a result of frustrations with regular broadband that hampered business processes and the ability to expand.

Prior to taking up the SFBB opportunity it was difficult for some SMEs to see the potential benefits of more reliable and faster connectivity, particularly when they had developed workarounds to deal with the problems they encountered on a daily basis as a result of poor bandwidth capability. However, the comments above show that experience is king in this context; hands-on experience of using SFBB heavily influenced the very positive views expressed regarding attitudes towards fibre connectivity and helped to overcome any apprehensions SME may have felt initially.

4.8   THE VIRTUOUS CIRCLE OF CONNECTIVITY

Participants were asked whether their experience of using SFBB had lived up to expectations and all reported that it had, and that they had become accustomed to improved SFBB connectivity very quickly:

> I had it pretty much 2 days after it came out in our town. I had it set up and that's a year and a bit now, you do take it for granted, you can just go bang and do it. Tourism and Hospitality

Not only had participants quickly become accustomed to faster speeds and greater bandwidth capacity, they also felt they had become increasingly reliant on better connectivity to run their businesses effectively. This far exceeded their reliance on previous broadband provision because it enabled them to do so much more:

> It depends on how embedded it is in your business but the more you use it, the more embedded it gets and the more you have to take that into consideration, particularly if you're moving home, premises or whatever. Fire and Flood Restoration

Some participants also reported having become more reliant on SFBB than they were on their previous broadband provision because it has enabled them to work in new and different ways that exploit the advantage of greater speeds and reliability:

> You are more reliant on Superfast Broadband than you were on regular broadband, without a doubt…you can do things now you'd never even considered before. Management Consultancy

SFBB has a pivotal role in delivering value through new-found efficiencies and savings. The comments above clearly illustrate SMEs' increased reliance on improved connectivity to run their businesses effectively and competitively. None of the participants we spoke to could conceive of giving up the benefits SFBB delivers and all spoke enthusiastically about further innovations and the possibility of access to FTTP.

We uncovered this virtuous circle of connectivity through a chain of interdependent benefits of SFBB that have become so important to SMEs that they have become far more reliant on fibre connectivity than they ever were on regular broadband. SFBB is not just an improved way of working; it is a different way of working. As SME reliance on SFBB benefits grows that increases and reinforces the value, new dependencies are forged and a new set of values and benefits emerges that are used to even greater effect.

4.9   SPEED AND EFFICIENCY BENEFITS OF SFBB

Having experienced SFBB the value it provides has become deeply embedded in SMEs daily work practices and processes. Although inevitably the advantages that SFBB provides overlap and in many cases are interdependent, they can largely be broken down into those concerning improved speed and efficiency, economic, social and environmental benefits.

The most obvious impact of SFBB for SMEs is on speed and efficiency and these are important factors since they impact on business productivity. Both were cited in the course of discussion as having a beneficial effect on business in terms of reduced frustration, the ability to complete tasks more efficiently, improved multitasking and accomplishing more in a shorter time frame:

> We do a lot of web design stuff, there's a lot of CMS systems which you build online rather than locally and you know, the transfer rate was far superior and made our life a lot more comfortable and a lot quicker, and it speeded up your time really. Creative Media and Design

Participants were aware that increased speed and efficiency in their work practices as a result of SFBB had led to an increase in productivity:

> It makes a massive difference . . . because if you are sending say 24 images of gold coins down to Australia, bang, they're gone! And then you can send

another 24 to another client, and then to another 24, you know, and being able to do that is just magnificent because it frees up time as well, you can get on and do other things. Retail

Participants also reported that faster and more effective communication resulted in faster decision-making and greater productivity:

> It's the speed of communication in both directions that brings about the decisions that can be made quicker and hopefully more effectively than before. Retail

The benefits SMEs describe, are most aware of, and are most easily articulated are a result of the way in which they use their connectivity for business. Those SMEs who were more bandwidth dependent were most likely to identify additional benefits over and above increased speed. In the course of discussions, it was clear that SFBB provides benefits that make working practices not just quantitatively better (i.e. faster), it provides qualitative improvements in terms of what can be accomplished.

4.10   INCREASED ABILITY TO MULTITASK

Several participants described how SFBB enabled them to multitask, affording opportunities to accomplish more in the same period of time and hence operate more effectively:

> It's not just simply run your business, you can multi-task. If you look at business news of the day for example, you can look at the videos while you are sending stuff, you can do all of that at the same time. Management Consultancy

The ability to multitask was also perceived as providing greater business agility and as promoting innovation and creativity:

> I think it's the immediacy of it, and if you like, the agility of it . . . being able to do several things at the same time has meant that I can free my brain up to do other things, to do more innovative things rather than doing the pedestrian things, because the pedestrian things I can now do very quickly. Architecture

The ability to multitask was also cited as making life simpler, less frustrating and more enjoyable:

> I suppose you could just listen to a bit a jazz while you were doing some business if you wanted to, because you can do seven functions at once…music while you work with Superfast Broadband! Tourism and Hospitality

The ability to operate more effectively enables SMEs to reach the next stage in business progression; it promotes growth and agility and impacts productivity.

4.11   Reversing the Shift – Offline to Online

In Phase 1 of our research, before SMEs had access to SFBB, many reported a shift from operating online to offline as a workaround to accommodate delivery of large files and this has been a source of major frustration. Fibre connectivity has reversed this shift and participants reported being able to accomplish more of their business operations online:

> Before I would have to put files on a disc and get them couriered up to London, it was the only way…now I just send them and whoosh, they're gone, job done! Publishing

The speed with which large files could be sent also contributed to cost savings. This occurred in two ways; it eliminated the necessity to send files by courier, often incurring expensive charges, and it meant that PCs no longer had to be left on all night to accommodate the sending of large files during less congested periods:

> I wonder how many people, if they had a big file to send, used to say 'I'll do that overnight' and they would leave their computer on and let it run over night. Now they don't have to because it's all done and when they have finished or they leave the office, they can actually switch everything off. Business Services

Productivity and efficiency gains are not the only benefits that SFBB affords however, SMEs described many additional economic, social and environmental advantages including business process restructuring, further cost savings, better collaboration and growth, as well as innovations that had not previously been envisaged.

4.12   Economic Benefits of SFBB

Many of the benefits of SFBB are interdependent much in the way that improved speed and efficiency interrelates with productivity gains and cost saving. Speed and efficiency are the most readily articulated benefits, but participants also spoke enthusiastically about a number and range of substantial advantages that translate into economic benefits.

4.12.1   *Reducing the Need to Travel*

SFBB helped to reduce costs by reducing the need to travel. This enabled participants to reduce overheads as well as enabling them to serve a greater number of customers in a given time period as a result:

> It's reduced my overheads on my truck a lot. If I was going to fix a computer, you can only charge a certain rate given the rates in Cornwall aren't that high, you go to fix a person's computer and there is only so much they will pay. So you drive from Penzance to all over the place, an hour or so driving, you are there for a couple of hours . . . so it's four hours work for one hours pay, but now I can just sit at home and do it from there, so it's taken out the whole travel element and I can do more people, more quickly. IT Management

Several participants also noted that reduced travel improved productivity as well affording greater convenience:

> One of my directors is involved in a lot of the training in the human resource side of the business. Before Superfast she had to make regular trips down to Cornwall which isn't an easy journey by any means. Now we just jump on Skype, it's that simple. A two hour training sessions is just that, it's not a day and then a hotel stay and travel back the next day. Business Services

One of the beneficial factors of better connectivity that contribute to the reduced need to travel is improved Internet telephony capability. A more reliable connection provides better collaboration opportunities for face-to-face meetings without the need to meet in person and this saves time and enhances efficiency:

> I am much more efficient being at home and online than I am whenever I have to travel, like to London for meetings. I might get three meetings and

then I am scrabbling around trying to find Wi-Fi so that I can answer my emails, whereas I can have six meetings and do all of my emails and everything else I need from the office with no problem at all. Management Consultancy

Several SMEs reported that a reduction in travel also improved their work/life balance:

Now I can manage two projects concurrently in different locations. I can have a project running in Serbia and one in Tajikistan at the same time and I can find out what's going on in both of them, rather than getting on a plane and disappearing for a week. Management Consultancy

SFBB not only enabled participants to save time on travelling and attendant costs but also reduced frustration and enabled them to work in a different and more effective way:

I think one of the things that has happened is that you can do business in a very different way. I mean certainly the sort of business I do, I could never have done from home in Cornwall. I would have had to have been up in London, dealing with people up there because they are the sort of people I interact with, yet now I can do it quite happily from my home office, so it is looking at a totally different way of doing things really. Management Consultancy

Being able to reduce travel provides a number of advantages over and above any financial gain; it provides additional convenience, improved efficiency, time saving and reduces carbon footprint.

4.12.2   Increased Collaboration Opportunities

We found a marked increase in collaboration opportunities as a result of SFBB and participants felt this was very beneficial to their business. All were collaborating more with SFBB than with previous broadband provision and all agreed they were now working with a wider network of people:

It has improved networking essentially, it has enabled people to communicate more effectively with other people, collaborate with people more efficiently if you like. Management Consultancy

Superfast Broadband has made a real difference to my business. Definitely. It has enabled me to make conference calls all over the world, and it has enabled me to have consistent communication, uninterrupted. It's brilliant. Land-based Services

The ease with which communication can take place with SFBB connectivity also had an effect on SME's ability to widen the circle of those with whom they collaborate and this was considered to be very important:

It makes for better working relationships. When we set up in 2004 the early stage of our business was going over to meet people face-to-face a lot more . . . whereas now we don't need to do that, we can do a lot of things straight away, immediately with Superfast. Education and Training

We also saw evidence of SMEs making more use of social media as a result of SFBB:

I never thought I'd be saying this but now that I'm using Facebook I feel that I'm more in touch with the customers I do business with . . . and it's not just customers, it's suppliers, it's a more informal way of staying in touch. I couldn't be bothered before with the connection going down all the time, it felt like too much trouble. Retail

Several participants reported now using social networking sites for business and all felt that this was a positive change in that it enabled them to collaborate beyond the boundaries of their business premises, helping them to build better relationships with suppliers and customers alike:

Social media has changed the way we communicate dramatically . . . it's the trend of communication now. Retail

Although some participants were using social media prior to the introduction of SFBB, they were unanimous in their assertion that the reliability of SFBB connectivity made it much easier and more effective:

The fact that I have got a reliable connection now makes it so much easier. Tourism and Hospitality

The way SMEs were communicating with customers, suppliers and colla-borators was changing and SFBB was facilitating that change, improving agility and responsiveness.

4.12.3   Changing Patterns of Employment

Some participants reported they could reduce overheads with SFBB because, as a result of being able to work faster and more efficiently, they needed fewer employees. None had made any redundancies but neither did they view SFBB as creating more jobs, at least in the short term. However, although none of our participants reported having created more jobs, several reported others they knew of taking on new employees as a result of SFBB:

> Personally I haven't taken on any more staff but I have clients who have. Management Consultancy

The reasons participants gave for not taking on more staff were twofold; they were able to be more efficient themselves as a result of better con-nectivity and were able to collaborate with, rather than employ others, as a result of SFBB:

> To some extent Superfast Broadband means that you don't have to employ people. Whereas if you were running this sort, or my sort of business 5 years ago, to run it to the level I run it at the moment I would probably have to have somebody else but I don't need it now because I can be so much more efficient online, I can involve my colleagues in other parts of the world. It's a bit like the old fashioned secretary, as soon as we got word processors you didn't need an old fashioned secretary because you all did your own. Management Consultancy

SFBB affords SMEs increased access to a wider skills base through greater opportunities for collaboration with a wider network of potential employ-ees. Some participants were of the opinion that this had already changed working practices and the way people are employed:

> That collaborative word has taken over from employee. Management Consultancy

It's not really relevant for me to say 'yes I am going to expand my little office set up' because I just go and get someone in to help for a specific task. Business Services

Participants said they were able to access the best and most appropriate skills from a skills base that might exist worldwide rather than be confined to those in their immediate vicinity who made need training or upskilling. This enabled SMEs to be more discriminating in who they employed and for how long in order to achieve a particular outcome, and it was common for them to describe taking on collaborators on short-term contracts.

Whether or not SFBB really will change the way people are employed remains to be seen but Cornwall has a vibrant community of SMEs who all agree that Cornwall is an attractive place to live and work. Setting up in business is one way that natives can remain in Cornwall but that potential also attracts incomers and returners. The introduction of fibre connectivity enhances the attraction of Cornwall still further and helps nullify the negative effects of poor road, rail and air infrastructure.

4.12.4   Increased Use of Cloud Services

As discussed above, increased bandwidth capacity is the vehicle that enables far greater use of Cloud services. As well as productivity Cloud services also had significant economic benefits for many businesses. They helped reduce overheads and capital spend and provided reliability, security and availability that all contribute to greater convenience. Many participants said use of Cloud services had only become possible with the introduction of fibre connectivity:

It has only just become worthwhile since we've had Superfast. Accountancy

Participants reported using Cloud services mostly for backup and storage but also processing power, for example, rendering on the Cloud rather than locally:

We used to leave some workstations on to do photorealistic renderings and even though they were very powerful computers it would take a heck of a long time to do a high quality rendering, I can do it in the Cloud now and it's done in a minute and half. Creative Media and Design

> A lot of companies like us use the Cloud for back up now, off site. IT Management

Participants reported increased use of applications such as Google Docs and Dropbox as a direct result of SFBB connectivity. Although these could have been used over regular broadband for many; poor connectivity made this too cumbersome a process. SFBB acted as a catalyst that provokes change in working practices as more possibilities are opened up through improved bandwidth capacity and greater reliability:

> I don't know if we could have done it without Superfast but until we got it we simply didn't think of it. Now we've just started playing with ideas. I don't think technically it would have been impossible without, maybe, maybe not...but it's Superfast that made us think of trying it. Tourism and Hospitality

Cloud services are emerging as a major disruptive force as a result of SFBB. In facilitating the use of Cloud services, SFBB offers SMEs the opportunity to revolutionise the way they work and compete far more effectively with their larger rivals. The Cloud enables SMEs to access services without the need to invest in expensive IT equipment and provides flexibility that was previously unattainable. The ease, convenience and cost savings Cloud services provide are likely to play an increasingly important role in SME IT operations and as use grows and evolves, it is likely that dependence on such services will increase.

4.12.5   Improved Business Agility

One of the most discussed advantages amongst participants was the way SFBB had improved business agility, flexibility and response times and again, this was linked to improved competitiveness:

> I think what it does is it enables us to make use of one of the edges that small, independent, self-employed companies tend to have which is agility. The big companies don't have that because the big companies have to rely upon process to ensure that quality is delivered and process tends to build in sclerosis and inertia. But now, because we have got Superfast Broadband we can actually turn round proposals very quickly and we can respond on what it is the client wants in a much more

responsive manner, and in a personal manner which actually, people tend to like. Business Services

Agility and responsiveness were perceived to be strong advantages that small businesses have over larger companies that are hampered by process and SFBB was viewed as increasing those qualities:

I deal with people on a one-to-one basis … if you are dealing with a large multi-national company they might not respond for some time, yet when you have someone who is going to respond to you instantly, that means everything. Even if you come back with the wrong solution, it's the speed at which you respond and communicate. A large multi-national company is not capable of that. Managerial Consultancy

Rapid response time is crucial to SMEs and participants reported that SFBB had the effect of raising their expectations of the response times of others with whom they were dealing:

The thing we hate the most as business people is the lack of response from other people, that is the worst thing in business. Financial Services

For us, in a way we are expecting a response a lot quicker because we are sending out the questions and we expect them to be on the same system as us. Creative Media and Design

Several participants reported frustration in dealing with those who do not respond quickly:

One big frustration is … you are sending out communications, you are responding instantly and you expect them to respond instantly, but they don't. You can't have virtual conversations with somebody that doesn't know how to use the kit or hasn't got it and I find, especially over in the west of the country, they haven't built up a way to react, or even use the broadband. Accountancy

They'll see a communication but they don't know that you are using Superfast, their inertia is still in place, especially with the big companies. Retail

It could be argued that some of the benefits and advantages partici-pants described could have been achieved with effective regular broad-band but the simple fact is that this was not an option for many SMEs.

Before the introduction of fibre connectivity, many participants were operating with below optimal connectivity and found it necessary to devise a series of workarounds to accommodate slow speeds and poor bandwidth.

SFBB has become a critical enabler for SMEs in Cornwall as illustrated by the incremental benefits over regular provision that make a compelling case for adoption. At the very least the provision of fibre connectivity has provided a level playing field and, given Cornwall's peripheral location, that is a valuable asset in itself, but SFBB has provided the region's SMEs with far more than that; it has enabled new and unexpected ways of working and opened avenues of collaboration that would have been otherwise impossible.

4.13   Social Benefits of SFBB

Just as participants were able to articulate the economic benefits of fibre connectivity, they also discussed a number of social benefits. These were centred on overcoming Cornwall's peripheral location, attracting inward investment, improved ability to operate a business in Cornwall, choosing SFBB enabled premises, improved work/life balance and potential for regeneration.

4.13.1   Overcoming Cornwall's Peripheral Location

As discussed earlier, Cornwall suffers from its remoteness and lack of effective road, rail and air infrastructure. However, participants claimed that SFBB has made location irrelevant and helped overcome many of these difficulties.

Some SMEs spoke of businesses they knew of that had recently been set-up as a direct result of the introduction of SFBB, or were likely to survive and flourish because of SFBB:

> I certainly know of…a lady who has come down and runs an Internet business, a shopping business…I think anything from that perspective…because then it doesn't really matter where you are…Location is irrelevant, it's great in the summer, she runs a small craft business but she does most of her business online. Business Services

> I know of shops that probably wouldn't survive without it because just the passing trade that they get is not enough, they also rely on mail order sales as

well, particularly niche businesses. There is one down road from us which does body boards and okay, they get a fair old sale during the peak season in the summer but their Internet side allows them to trade at a healthy level all year round, so the shop survives. Retail

One participant stretched the idea of location being irrelevant to maintaining his business operations from his holiday venue:

My case is a bit different – I have just spent five days in Majorca and I could carry on working as if I was in the office from a laptop, and nobody was any the wiser. I transferred the phones to over there and because I made sure that I didn't actually have to meet anyone for those four days I was away, my clients were none the wiser. Management Consultancy

Participants were of the opinion that SFBB could open up markets to them that had been inaccessible before due to poor connectivity and were optimistic that as a direct result of fibre connectivity, businesses in the region had a new lease of life and far greater potential for growth and success.

4.13.2 Opportunities for Inward Investment

Many participants were optimistic about opportunities for inward investment to Cornwall created by SFBB:

I moved here from the Far East and I didn't know anyone within 200 miles when I arrived. I selfishly hope that Superfast attracts more people to relocate in the county. I feel very privileged to have sort of fluked finding such a great place and I hope more people come, they should do, not just artisans, but more small businesses. Land-based Services

We can create little hubs for them whether it's Bodmin or Redruth; all these places are vibrant now with fibre. I hope it doesn't affect the quaintness and the charm of the place but it could be a real step forward and attract more like-minded small businesses. Creative Media and Design

Although some felt this might take time to materialise:

I don't think fibre broadband is going to turn Cornwall into a super county, not yet, but you can work more efficiently and you can download files and you can do Skype efficiently, but it's not going to change Cornwall that much. We need investment, if bigger companies move to Cornwall that would be great. Business Services

A small minority felt that the opportunity for inward investment only existed while Cornwall had a head start in fibre connectivity ahead of other areas in the UK but comments were still positive:

> I think that chance has gone for inward investment because the whole of the country will have it very shortly, but it will be a great equaliser. Financial Services

Cornwall is traditionally a holiday destination and several SMEs said that they would like to see a move away from a business emphasis on tourism and services for tourists and felt that SFBB offered an opportunity for that to happen through inward investment:

> At the start I was in the holiday trade, but I would like to see as much emphasis put onto other business interests in Cornwall. A little over a third of the income coming into the county is via the holiday trade but as a business person I'm looking over my shoulder saying 'what's happening to the other two thirds?' There's a lot of chances being missed if we just concentrate on tourism, I think it's blinkered, we need to look at other industries, there's room for both. Management Consultancy

Others said that inward investment would provide them with the opportunity to broaden their own customer base, and cited examples of how SFBB had already made this possible:

> There is a girl in our village, we are like just outside Truro, there is a girl there selling sailing bags and things like that but prior to that she wasn't doing very much at all. Her business has really took off and she is obviously on Superfast as well, but I think people are moving down and setting up businesses here knowing that they can get Superfast Broadband. Retail

> I can make money out of America, I use a site in New Orleans and sell stuff so that just gives you another income stream, I don't have to be in Cornwall to do that ... but you do need Superfast. Retail

Some participants felt that fibre connectivity alone made enough of a difference to Cornwall to attract new businesses that might be considering relocation. Others felt that it was still dependent on better road and rail infrastructure and that this required development first:

> The only way you'll attract business here is to actually improve the infrastructure to bring industry in., the physical infrastructure needs improving. We need that to get businesses to relocate. Land-based Services

> I think high fuel prices make Cornwall a bit more inaccessible, the roads, the rail and flying, the prices are just going up and up. So, in terms of attracting inward investment which relies on moving things, or people, we are just too far away, and that's down to the cost. Anything beyond Bristol or Exeter, people don't believe it's there, There's dual carriageway to Plymouth, then it stops and the same with Launceston. Management Consultancy

Some were also concerned that Cornwall might not have the right skill set to attract inward investment:

> At the moment it's a lifestyle choice to live down here, you are not going to have that many big companies coming down on a lifestyle choice; you have to have the infrastructure and the skill sets. Creative Media and Design

SMEs were very keen that any inward investment opportunities should be exploited and that they should encompass a move away from tourism and the service industry to provide better paid jobs and opportunities in the region.

4.13.3   Improved Work/Life Balance

Very few of our participants reported working fewer hours as a result of SFBB, in fact the reverse was true for some who maintained that better connectivity meant they were always available. However, all said they could accomplish more and that this could be achieved more efficiently and effectively. As a result, participants said that SFBB had reduced their frustration, created greater convenience and improved their quality of life:

> It's not really improved the business but it's made me happy. Funeral Services

There is no question, it is less frustrating, you switch it on and it's there, there's no frustration at all now, you can work when you want to. Land-based Services

Although many participants said they used the time saved in working faster to accomplish additional tasks, a minority said it simply gave them more leisure time:

The time I save working I spend stroking the cat mostly! Management Consultancy

I look at You Tube videos, read the news, things I wouldn't have time for normally, I probably waste more time. Tourism and Hospitality

It's easier to do business when it's faster and I spend less hours at the machine in the evening, having done a day's work, than I used to. Management Consultancy

Other participants suggested that the improved opportunity SFBB provides to work from home would have a positive impact on work/home balance and the local economy:

If people can work from home now they will do, and they can do that and live in Cornwall, that's always been the case. When I came to Cornwall in the early '70s there were a few people doing that but Superfast means more people can come and live here and work remotely, I think Superfast will encourage that. It will be good for them in terms of health and lifestyle and good for us because they will be spending money in the local economy. Creative Media and Design

The ability to work from home was cited as having a major impact on improving work/life balance but for many this had only become viable when SFBB became available. A minority of participants were unable to access SFBB from their business premises but had access at home and said that their working pattern had changed to spending more time at home as a result.

4.13.4   Increased Flexibility in Working Hours

In Phase 1 of our research, discussed in Chap. 3, many SMEs told us that they worked very late at night or got up as early as 4 am to accomplish bandwidth heavy tasks that would have been impossible in the course of normal working hours due to contention ratio problems. SFBB has enabled many to normalise their working hours providing the bandwidth capacity they need whenever it is required resulting in speedier and more efficient working practices.

Participants reported that being able to conduct business more reliably with SFBB improved flexibility in working hours. They were no longer hampered by having to avoid heavily congested periods of Internet activity when children came home from school, during school holidays or during evenings and weekends.

> It's enabled us to be a bit more flexible with working hours. Motor Trade

> Before the quality of service degenerated towards the end of the afternoon, but that doesn't happen now ... it's a bit like a dial tone, it's available whenever you want it, so that means you can plan your day without reference to that, which means you can be much more flexible. Land-based Services

> I can do whatever I need to do whenever I need to do it, I'm not waiting around until the early hours or whatever to claw back some bandwidth. Creative Media and Design

SMEs also reported being able to accomplish more through greater flexibility in working hours, although in several cases participants reported that this resulted in working for longer:

> I just find, because of the speed of the thing, I actually work longer days because I want to get stuff out because you never know what is coming in the door or down the wire at some other stage during the day. Management Consultancy

> I get up at 6 am instead of 7 am now and spend an hour just clearing the decks ... it's too convenient! Accountancy

Much of the improved flexibility that participants described was as a result of greater reliability and bandwidth capacity:

> I don't have Superfast at home yet, I have it at work, but one of the things I do at home is audio editing and I finished a CD and somebody wanted it in London urgently so I finished it at home and I got it to them quicker by

taking my laptop to work, driving 4 miles to work, connecting it to the broadband and uploading it from there. Creative Media and Design

Such flexibility is largely perceived to be an advantage, but we did find some evidence of the evolution of a 24-hour culture as a result of changed expectations created by more reliable connectivity:

The downside, from my wife's point of view, is getting ridiculous phone calls at silly o'clock in the morning and they want their machine up and running before the start of their business day... people expect you to be there on call when they need you and that can be 2 in the morning on a Sunday. IT Management

It's the speed at which information is being given to you now... people are more reliant on it... Financial Services

Greater reliability and flexibility in working hours was particularly appreciated by those working across different time zones:

It's the consistency of the signal, your connectivity is there, it's guaranteed. The great thing about that is you have got the flexibility to do it any time of day so you are not restricted by time zones if you don't mind getting up. Management Consultancy

This represents a great change in working practices for SMEs who told us in Phase 1 of the research that they worked unsocial hours on a regular basis, trying to pick periods of least Internet congestion so that they could accomplish tasks that were otherwise impossible. The fact that participants had so much to say about the ability to work more flexibly as a result of SFBB also indicates how important this is as a benefit.

4.14 Environmental Impact

In the course of discussions, participants gave many examples of working differently with SFBB that have an environmental impact. Even though participants rarely couched the advantages of using Cloud services, Skype, working from home or reduced travel in terms of improving their green credentials, these opportunities have the potential to reduce SME's carbon footprint.

We gave SMEs the opportunity to talk about the environmental impact of using SFBB and how it might contribute to sustainability issues but found scant evidence of concern, only a minority were interested in this aspect:

> I think it is vitally important to care about our planet; it's all we have got. Architecture

> I use 100 % renewable electricity which costs more but I prefer to pay and feel I'm doing my bit. Creative Media and Design

> I don't think you can ignore the cutting the carbon footprint thing really. Every time you book an airline ticket it's there asking if you'd like to offset, so yeah, it does bother me. Land-based Services

The following comments were more typical of contributions to the discussion:

> Chop the tree down, smack it up in the corner and burn it the following year, that's about as green as I get. Motor Trade

> I don't think the carbon footprint is our major concern. Management Consultancy

> I don't feel that great social responsibility … For me, the benefits of being able to use the technology are in terms of my lifestyle. That's the bottom line, not in being socially responsible, I like to think we do things ethically but social responsibility is not a primary concern. Digital Services

The type of business in which participants were engaged also influenced whether they considered SFBB could help them make any savings on their carbon footprint. For example, a participant engaged in building and plumbing told us:

> Not for me in any way, shape or form has Superfast reduced my carbon footprint. I used to work from home but now 90 % of what I do is physical, I have to come to your house and put a new boiler in or put a new roof on and I can't do that from home. Plumbing/Construction

For most participants any carbon saving was overshadowed by an emphasis on the economic aspects and how SFBB could save on overheads, rather than impact on the environment:

> I think the cost of the petrol is more of a concern … most people would say the price of petrol, if you can save a couple of trips … IT Management

> I think they go hand in hand but really it's a case of, if I don't need to go there, it saves me the cost in fuel, but it's nothing to do with social responsibility, it's to do with personal comfort. Management Consultancy

Whether or not SMEs were concerned with environmental issues and how SFBB might help reduce their carbon footprint, there were several instances where a positive impact might occur, even though this was not readily articulated by participants.

4.14.1   Potential for Reduced Carbon Footprint through Less Travel

Many participants reported a reduced need to travel as a result of fibre. Several factors contributed to this: the ability to access information online, better and more effective Skype communication and working from home:

> Before we would have travelled to archive and record offices but there is a lot more information online now so that's probably cut our travel, a slight decrease I'd say. Business Services

> There was always a lot of travelling involved in my job but there's less now because we can do a lot more from home. IT Management

Some participants were of the opinion that any carbon savings as a result of a reduction in travel were likely to be minimal because they had already organised their lives and businesses to minimise fuel costs as a direct result of rising fuel prices. Again, motivations were focused on economic rather than sustainability issues:

> A lot of us are working from home anyway. For myself, my office is only three miles from my home so my mileage is very low. I wanted it that way anyway so it was close to pick up the kids from school and also the cost of fuel was rising so it just makes life a lot easier. Personally I don't think it will help with my carbon footprint. The odd meeting, the odd time when I might have to go to Devon to a site where they can show me the issues yes, but that could be a couple of times a month, that's all. Digital Services

One group of participants felt that the opportunities SFBB provides for business expansion had actually increased their carbon footprint and they were travelling more than they had formerly:

> Maybe it's very particular to our business but because of the ability we now have to share documents and photos, we can now send a technician to London, or Birmingham, or Newcastle, so they are now driving to

Birmingham, Newcastle and London whereas before we were much more regionally based around Cornwall and Devon and that was it really. Getting paperwork back and then data processing it to get the reports out would never have been possible before, so Superfast has enabled us to increase our range of work and out of it all we are driving far more miles. Fire and Flood Restoration

Better connectivity creates opportunities for some, but by no means all SMEs, to reduce their need to travel. Inevitably, a reduction in travel helps reduce the carbon footprint but few participants mentioned this, instead they told us how it enabled them to save on fuel and accommodation costs. This suggests that appeals to SMEs sense of social responsibility in regard to sustainability may best be focused on economic aspects.

4.15   ISSUES AND CONCERNS

In the course of discussion, a number of issues and concerns around SFBB arose. Some of these were focused around a skills and knowledge gap in using IT and how fibre connectivity is delivered. Others were concerned with a perceived slowing down of SFBB speeds since participants had originally signed up. We also found a greater dependence on fibre connectivity that arises from the benefits of being able to work differently that increase SMEs sense of vulnerability.

4.15.1   Skills Gap

In today's fast-moving digital economy, technical skills are vital to business growth and success. Whilst participants were confident they had the skills to run their business effectively, a high proportion said they were not technically proficient:

I don't know any technical stuff; I'm just running an office and a business. Motor Trade

People try and explain what the problem is and I say 'look, I just want it fixed, I don't want to understand why.' It's often just little things . . . Tourism and Hospitality

Most SMEs knew of someone they could call on to fix computing problems or deal with technical difficulties:

> I'm sure I could be more efficient if I knew what things were called and what they did but I just don't, you know? I just get somebody else in to sort it out for me. I just haven't got the patience to sit there and do it even though it could be that some things are quite simple, or I get some of the young staff to come in and sort it out for me. Tourism and Hospitality

> If something goes wrong, I've got a little man that comes and fixes it. He came in the other day and he said 'your systems needs upgrading, I'll come in Friday, take them home for the weekend and bring them back first thing on Monday morning.' It's more RAM, upgrade to Windows 7…and I think, just go away and do it and bring it back, and if it works faster, I'll be happier. Education and Training

None of our participants considered their lack of technical expertise to be a hindrance to making the most of what SFBB has to offer and few were of the opinion that they needed new skills to take advantage of SFBB:

> Yesterday I was on ISDN, then I moved to ADSL, skills required? Change nil. Then I've gone from ADSL to Superfast and Infinity 2 and there's still no change in the skills I need. Business services

> Superfast shouldn't make any difference at all to your security, your skills or whatever, else; it just makes the ability to do it quicker. Retail

Some participants felt that any additional skill requirements would only become necessary if they changed their field of business but even then, those skills were likely to be associated with the new field of operations rather than skills to use IT kit and fibre connectivity more effectively:

> It depends entirely what you are going to use it for, if you're going to try and go into another area of expertise then you may need to develop additional skills, but not to run my business now. Creative Media and Design

It is interesting to note that, almost without exception, only those participants who were engaged in the IT industry felt that there was a skills gap in the SME community:

There's a massive gap I think. IT Management

Most people have limited technical knowledge and they are not interested in general. It's not everyone, some pay an interest in the technology and they know how to log into their router or whatever, but by and large people are not that technical, they don't have the skills IT Management

It was difficult to gauge participants' skills level because in the course of discussion we had to rely on self-report. However, comments of those participants who worked in the computing industry or served the computing needs of fellow SMEs suggest that there may be more of a skills gap than SMEs are aware. Although SMEs are very good at running their businesses effectively, many do not have the technical skills to diagnose what has gone wrong when problems arise, or knowledge of the technical terms to describe their problem to a help desk. For some SMEs, the belief that they know enough to operate effectively hampers any upskilling potential and hinders growth. In many cases, participants were not aware of what it is that they do not know; hence they do not recognise a skills gap. Others, who have no interest in gaining technical skills, bring in expertise as and when it is needed and some are so busy running their business that they do not feel they have the time to address matters themselves.

4.15.2 Knowledge Gap

In Phase 1 of our research, we found a distinct knowledge gap amongst SMEs in understanding the differences between broadband delivery over copper and delivery over fibre. In the course of Phase 2 discussions, it became apparent that there is still a degree of misunderstanding about how SFBB is delivered. For example, we found evidence that participants still believed that distance from the exchange impacts on SFBB speed:

Mine is round about 24 megs but that's due to the distance from the exchange. Business Services

It's all on old technology, that's where you start to get the different speeds, the distant from the exchange, but also it is all still linking up to old technology. Financial Services

It was also clear from other comments made by participants that they do not understand how fibre technology works:

> What I have never understood is why it is that Superfast broadband, when they first install it, you get told what speed it is and the engineer will then say 'it will take a while whilst it settles down.' It's not logical, if it's a connection it's either there or it's not...nobody will ever tell you why. Funeral Directors

Confusion regarding how the technology works led a number of participants to voice concerns about how to trace what had gone wrong when faults occur:

> When it fails we don't know where it fails, or in what way it fails, and I think all around here we are probably using a new technology which we don't quite understand. We may be using it before it's really fit for use, you plug the kettle in at home and you expect it to work and it's the same with your telly...but with this there's lots of boxes to join up with lots of bits of wire and when it fails I'm at a loose end working at home, I don't know where it has failed, but it happens too often for me to just dismiss it as once in a blue moon. Financial Services

Those participants engaged in IT support elucidated further on knowledge gaps they had uncovered in their dealings with SME clients and the impact that had on perceptions of what might have gone wrong, or what is causing systems to slow down:

> I went to a customer the other day and he said the computer was running very slowly at a certain time of day. They weren't even aware that their actual back-up was running then, that's why his computer was slow! There's lots of scenarios like that...that the customers don't know about so you know, it's like they are blind-folded...they haven't got a clue. IT Management
>
> A lot of small businesses in Cornwall just don't have the budget to upgrade, that's why so many are still running Windows XP which is expiring next year and lots of businesses aren't aware of it...I don't think they understand how efficient it can make them and how much more productive they could be. I think it's a knowledge thing rather than they don't want to. IT Management

Participants tended to dismiss technical knowledge as unimportant or not their area of expertise, but discussions revealed that a lack of basic knowledge about what might impact connection speed does impact on business. The most common misunderstanding was how using a wireless rather than an Ethernet connection would considerably reduce the speed of operation:

> I got a 17 meg download speed when I did the speed test and I thought 'oh, that's a bit bad' because it was over our 40 meg connection. So I went to a colleague's PC and he got 38 or something, it was because I was on wireless and I hadn't realised…so it was interesting that it was half the speed. Publishing

Contributions to the discussion from those engaged in the IT support business also confirmed that common misconceptions regarding impacts on speed abound:

> There's quite a lot of misconception, there's a lot of customers out there who think if they get Superfast Broadband it will speed up their computer, and of course, it doesn't. There's a lot of people out there that think 'if I go for fibre broadband my computer will be so much better' and really of course, it isn't. IT Management

4.15.3 Increased Dependency on SFBB Perceived to Increase Vulnerability

Earlier in this chapter, we described how SMEs are becoming increasingly dependent on the benefits and added value that SFBB provides and how this leads to a virtuous circle of connectivity. The more SMEs use SFBB, the more value they derive and the more dependent on fibre connectivity and the advantages it provides they become. As a result of the benefits participants discover, they are able to work differently and this provides a route to further innovation and greater dependence on the vehicle through which this is made possible – fibre connectivity. Participants were very aware of their growing dependence on SFBB and this led many to voice the perception that this increased their vulnerability if access was compromised, and the potential risks to their business of losing connectivity:

> My concern is, if my business expands . . . my major need of the Internet and the speed I get now is for morning conferences to communicate with other people. As the business grows bigger and I have got more and more diverse people to contact, will the system slow up and crash? That is my big concern. Financial Services

Given that participants believed that SFBB had slowed down since they first signed up and that this was due to competition for bandwidth resources, several voiced concerns regarding whether current SFBB speeds were sustainable. Many believed that as more and more people take up the fibre option, speeds will diminish:

> I am particularly concerned . . . at the moment, we may be lucky, we may be the only people using fibre but I think we'll notice when others come on, it will go down. Tourism and Hospitality

> I have been expecting that it will slow down as more people come on. Business Services

Participants were worried that as time goes on they may have to compete more heavily with consumers as an increasing number of bandwidth hungry services are delivered over SFBB:

> I want reassurance I suppose, as somebody who has taken up Superfast Broadband, that large organisations are not going to be allowed to swamp it and thereby destroy it. If we take the BBC, it is trying to persuade people to take television through broadband, if 300,000 homes in Cornwall watch their TV through our fibre links will it be Superfast anymore, or will it just grind to a halt? Financial Services

> That's the reassurance we need isn't it, that they will not come back and say to us in 10 years' time 'well you can have a faster link but you will have to pay three times as much for it,' I mean as a business customer, so you don't have to compete with YouTube or iPlayer or whatever they come up with next. Business Services

Participants felt that a further contributory factor to compromised SFBB speeds in the future may be as a result of more people opting to work from home as SFBB becomes more widely available:

With more and more people working from home, which is where the trend is going, you are going to have more and more resources being used. Digital Services

This was particularly pertinent to many of our participants who already worked from home and suspected others would follow suit. Many were convinced that this would compromise SFBB speeds even further and negatively impact the reliability they value:

The apprehension I have got is that my businesses relies on morning online conferences all over the country. Is it going to crash and not work? Financial Services

Participants who had devised new processes and different ways of working as a result of SFBB were the most reliant on the new capability it offers, but were also the most concerned about any possible degeneration in service. For most, these fears were focused on not knowing what the limits might be:

For us it is an unknown quantity if I am honest with you, because we have started so many processes which I don't think would have been possible before SFBB, so there has kind of come a point where we are using it for so much, we are going to start testing its limits. We have recently gone over to using Google docs for sharing images; we have got quite a lot of technicians in the field constantly sending us quite large images of properties back continuously . . . we are having Skype conversations going on too. What my worry is, when will we hit the limit and what is its capability – that is an unknown quantity we don't know until we hit it and then it's going to be like, what do we do now? It is that unknown quantity which is concerning me and something to be aware of. Fire and Flood Restoration

Access to SFBB has changed perceptions of what can be achieved and delivered for both business customers and consumers and this puts additional pressure on fibre infrastructure to deliver. Changing perceptions of what is possible and a growing reliance on fibre connectivity to accomplish business growth also places additional pressure on SMEs. It is interesting that participants were already considering the impact that a compromised service may have on business and this emphasises the value they place on the difference fibre connectivity has made. Whilst it is likely that knowledge gaps contribute to some SME concerns, other possibly more legitimate fears could be addressed through appropriate business packages that offer fail-safe reliability, and an optimum guaranteed level of service provided this is offered at an acceptable price point.

4.15.4   *Communicating with Those Who Do Not Have SFBB*

One issue that participants had experienced was frustration in trying to deal with other areas of the UK or other countries that did not have access to fibre connectivity, or dealing with those who had not taken-up the opportunity. Most of these problems involved trying to send large files:

> The only problem we are all getting is when we send big files to people, when we send video for example, which we can, we can send video to anywhere in the world now. The problem is whether or not they can actually receive that at the speed at which we can send. Creative Media and Design

> I find when you are working with other countries that there is a bottle neck with the country you work with because they don't have sufficient bandwidth...you can send very large files and basically they are on dial-up in Mozambique or whatever, and they just can't receive it. Management Consultancy

Such problems exist even in dealing with government departments and for some participants this had created difficulties:

> It's not just that they can't accept that amount of data, some people refuse to...a lot of our work now, rather than producing paper copies of things and depositing planning applications and business regulations applications, we actually deposit online. Yet the planning portal, which is government sponsored, where you can deposit planning applications, can only accept a 25 megabyte upload which is pathetic, and therefore you cannot use your advantage of producing amazing things, like doing photo lift realistic renderings using Cloud computing and incorporating that in a deposit, because their system won't take it. Architecture

> It does mean that you have got a disadvantage because you cannot communicate with all of the people who haven't got it. Transport

Others reported difficulties in using Skype with those without access to SFBB:

It is really frustrating because when it works it's fantastic and you can have 2 or 3 conversations going on between the office and Plympton or Birmingham, it's fantastic but yeah, that is the limiting thing when the other party hasn't got Superfast and hopefully in time it will resolve itself. Financial Services

Some participants talked about the reverse situation being true for those who had even greater fibre connectivity in other countries, dealing with those who "only" had SFBB:

What about the people in Japan or China who have this amazingly fast speed, how do they feel when they are contacting to people here who only have Superfast? Creative media and design

I was in Tokyo a few years ago and I had to send a 40 meg file back to Cornwall. I went on to YouSendIt and it said the programme is updated so do you want to update, so I updated it and sent the file and it was whoosh, gone! I thought blimey, this is fantastic, so when I got onto the net and looked at the hotel we were in it had like a 50 meg connection, so at the time it was just incredible. Management Consultancy

Although participants were frustrated in dealing with companies and government departments that did not have SFBB, most participants were aware of Cloud-based options such as Dropbox to help overcome these difficulties, even if they were not considered to be ideal:

There are systems out there now where you can upload a file and they can go to that particular site and download it. Education and Training

That slows the procedure down a bit because then they have to go to that place to retrieve the information. . . . Fire and Flood Restoration

But not everybody thought this was an effective solution:

I can't say this can be done through Hotmail, they'll say, "tough mate!" They won't accept it! Business Services

As the quote above suggests, "it's about the rest of the world catching up" and although this is causing some difficulties at present, it is actually a good problem to have. As indeed "the rest of the world" does catch up and switches to fibre connectivity, the problem is likely to disappear.

4.16 CONCLUSION

To date, most of the studies concerning the introduction of fibre connectivity have focused on fibre access infrastructure. There are very few studies of the advantages that fibre connectivity offers to SMEs over and above operating faster and more efficiently, hence this study helps to fill that gap. As findings from Phase 1 of our research suggested, there is a great appetite among business in Cornwall for improved broadband speeds and the consistency and reliability that fibre can deliver. Our research indicates an exceedingly positive outcome of upgrading to SFBB for rural SMEs, even though our sample had only had access for up to 12 months.

We uncovered new and unexpected ways of working in the SME community as a result of taking up the SFBB opportunity, and a number of benefits that span a range of businesses processes. Our findings suggested a significant impact of SFBB that is already playing a key role in increasing SME competiveness and agility, and stimulating productivity, growth and enhanced business innovation. Even though the shift from ordinary broadband to fibre connectivity is less tangible than the switch from dial-up to broadband, for many SMEs it represents the same kind of step change. Whereas the move from dial-up to broadband created a change in the way the Internet is accessed, the move from broadband to fibre has changed what is accessed and how SMEs use the greater connectivity it provides. SFBB is not just quantitatively better, it is qualitatively improved.

In the next chapter, we look at long-term impacts from those businesses who, by the end of the project, had the technology for more than 18 months, looking more specifically at long-term impacts such as changes to business practice and new developments.

CHAPTER 5

Always Wanting More

Abstract Phase 3 research further highlighted the virtuous circle of connectivity, showing the longer-term use of fibre connectivity (18 months plus) resulted in it becoming an essential part of the organisation, allowing new ways of working, the exploitation of virtual workforces, down- and rightsizing businesses, expanding customer base and reaching worldwide markets and business diversification. However, the research also highlighted the fundamental, almost business critical, role connectivity now played in organisations and their total reliance upon it for business success, meaning the reliability was crucial to the services. It also highlighted further needs for skills gaps to be addressed and that perceived benefits, such as environmental impact, perhaps are not as clear as first assumed.

Keywords Fibre connectivity · SMEs · Rural business · Business diversification · Virtual workforces · Skills gap

In this chapter exploring our data in detail, we report on the final phase of a longitudinal study of small/medium enterprises (SMEs) experience of fibre connectivity. Phase 3 of this research aimed to gauge the impact of Superfast Broadband (SFBB) for SMEs in the successful and effective running of businesses in Cornwall after they have had access to SFBB for 18 months. Given the longer-term

© The Author(s) 2017
A. Phippen, H. Lacohée, *The Impact of Fibre Connectivity on SMEs,*
DOI 10.1007/978-3-319-47554-7_5

adoption of the technology with this group of businesses, we hoped to explore and understand how nascent and novel innovations, collaborations and different ways of working have developed with longer experience of use. This phase of the research focused on the following:

- Whether SFBB has continued to meet SMEs aspirations and expectations over time;
- Whether speed and efficiency benefits of SFBB have endured;
- Enduring business impacts and ability to work differently as a result of access to;
- SFBB;
- SME innovation as a result of SFBB;
- SME's ability to maximise SFBB benefits;
- SME's future aspirations and future proofing;
- Connectivity options and Fibre to the Premise (FTTP);
- SME issues and concerns.

5.1   INTRODUCTION

The research reported here was Phase 3 of a longitudinal SME study of fibre connectivity and focused on changes to business as a result of using SFBB that have developed and endured over an 18 month period of use.

Phase 3 was concerned with comparing and contrasting how benefits are accrued over time and are compounded by those discovered in the earlier stages of adoption. Whereas the move from dial up to broadband created a change in the *way* the Internet is accessed, the move from broadband to fibre has changed *what* is accessed and how SMEs use the greater connectivity it provides. SFBB is not just quantitatively better, it is qualitatively improved and in Phase 3 we investigated how these changes have evolved and the impact they have on running a business.

5.2   SFBB AND SME EXPECTATIONS

Discussions began with a focus on whether SFBB has continued to meet participants' expectations. As this phase of the research was concerned with those who had been using SFBB for 18 months or more, our participants were those who had taken-up the opportunity as soon as fibre was available. This was not because they were early adopters, but because they were keen to overcome the problems of poor connectivity and having used SFBB over the course of 18 months, participants described it as "life changing":

> You're only limited now by your own creativity, rather than the technology. Marketing

> With my business, my sound, my TV business, it completely changed my life almost overnight. I used to download a whole load of files to a mate in Bristol where I used to work, sometimes 2, 3 GB, most of the time that was the size limit you could send. I'd get given the same amount of work as somebody in…the amount of time to do a job as somebody who was in Bristol, but I had to allocate myself 24 hours to load the files back to Bristol, and then overnight that went down to 40 minutes, so it was just complete-ly…phenomenal. So instead of staying up all night pretending I was in Bristol, I suddenly had a life again. I've got 20 MB upload which is fine for what I do. Sound Engineer

As in Phase 2, participants said they had become used to the improve-ments they experienced with SFBB very quickly:

> You take it for granted. You know, it works, it's kind of like electricity, you turn on the switch, it works, you just plug into the Wi-Fi or you could browse the web without it buffering, you know? Digital Services

In Phase 3, many talked about their experience of using SFBB as evolution rather than revolution:

> The biggest thing from my point of view is not something that I suddenly realise, "Oh, I can do that now," it's sort of gradually evolved in so far as I rely on having about 15 or 20 web pages open. One might be help files for the software I'm using; one might be a forum that I'm on. Another one might be my web-mail, you know, loads and loads of stuff. Digital Services

> You get used to it gradually evolving. You don't realise the change it has made to the way you work and the way you do business…Sometimes you have to think hard about whether it's made a difference or not, but it's only when you think about it that you realise that it probably has. I mean-…undoubtedly. Financial Services

Participants were also very aware of the degree to which their businesses now depend on fibre connectivity and this had increased since Phase 2 when participants had only used it for 6–12 months:

> It's just like the air we breathe, the water we drink, it's so important to business, to private life, to anything. . . . e-Commerce Website Developer

> I'd rather have it than not have it! I wouldn't be without it. Financial Services

> This is our HS2. Tourism

As predicted in Phase 2, Phase 3 showed evidence that SFBB availability had a strong influence on business location; participants were unanimous in their opinion that SFBB availability was top of their list of requirements for business premises:

> Oh absolutely, it will influence where we relocate to. Management Consultancy

> We've already looked at one set of premises and that was one of the things we did, we checked, just on the postal code, to find out if the broadband, if fibre optic was available there. I mean it would be a backward step if we went to somewhere that didn't have it. I think this is the problem probably for all of us, that you're spoilt now. If you were to move somewhere else you wouldn't go somewhere without Superfast, and there was something in the paper recently about estate agents are now including it in their details, because people want to know. Digital Services

Because reliable connectivity was now more vital to running a business than ever before, others have adopted or are considering adopting a "belt and braces" approach by running two broadband services side by side to ensure connectivity. It was interesting to note that this was a solution that some SMEs had employed in Phase 1 of our research with regular broadband to safeguard against loss of service. In Phase 2 with SFBB users of 6–12 months, participants said this necessity had become redundant because fibre connectivity was perceived to be much more reliable than regular broadband. Now, in Phase 3 we were seeing a return to this practice, not because SFBB was considered to be unreliable, but because connectivity has become even more business critical.

We actually run two broadbands side by side, one being a standard speed and one from BT, one with Superfast. We run two at the same time. Leisure and Tourism

We're too reliant on connectivity so we're looking at having double the Internet connections too, like a failsafe. You cannot afford to be isolated from the outside world for a long period of time. Creative Design

Several participants told us that fibre connectivity "does what it says on the box", that is, it enables SMEs to accomplish what they want to do online without having to worry about reliability or slow connections breaking down. For SMEs, this meant that they no longer had to consider whether or not their broadband connection will "work" and this helped to build confidence and a sense of the technology becoming:

You do it now without thinking, whereas before, if you wanted to just email somebody a photo it took half the day, you know? Now, you can send a dozen photos and it just goes and it's just, small things like that just make it simpler and quicker and easier, and we do more research online than we used to. Historical Research

We also found many instances where participants told us that fibre connectivity had enabled businesses to remain located in Cornwall, and some noted that those outside of the region are becoming aware of Cornwall's greater connectivity:

You'll be awarded a contract based on the merits of delivering it. So then when you've won it they go, "Oh, I didn't know you were in Cornwall." I'm like, 'Is that an issue?' "No." People are being re-educated to that, you know? But you've also got to support it with confidence you can deliver. It does mean that when you're operating systems like this they have to work, they can't let you down. Creative Design

For many, SFBB was a must for the home as well as the office as described by one participant who had moved the business from home-based to office-based premises:

When I moved from home-based to an office, I moved the Superfast to the office and I thought, "You know what? I don't need the expense of Superfast at home; I'll just get normal broadband." But for home use . . . using iPlayer etc., it wasn't any good and to, well, to put it bluntly, my wife turned around to me and said, "Get the Superfast back!" It's when you take it away that you notice the difference. e-Commerce Website Development

In Phase 3, we found that rather than moving from home based to office based as in the case above, more SMEs were giving up their business premises to relocate at home as a result of SFBB. Some participants described having completely changed their working practices, either working solely from home or via remote access:

I can work from home entirely now, I don't have to go out. Digital Services (music)

For me, because I was providing IT support, I can log in to a lot of my client's machines remotely. It's cheaper, so that's better for me, I still go out, if there is a problem, I will still go out, but they just love the fact that I can log in and sort it out. It's quick. Digital Services (IT Support)

Some participants had given up their business premises as a result of improved efficiency with SFBB:

We don't have to have so many people out on the road now, I used to have a shop in the town and I used to have guys there but now, I've retreated back to the home and found it has not been a problem. Digital Services (IT Support)

The option to work from home was not greeted as a positive move by all however, and some described advantages of working from office premises:

I was working at home for three years and I have just moved into an office and it is one of the best things that I have done because it has formed some separation, and home is a nicer place to go to now, whereas before it was still work. Digital Services and Wine Merchant

Others noted family issues when working from home:

I'm definitely suffering from that, especially when I have bands in recording – that being an issue with her indoors. It's harder to switch off but that doesn't bother me. Digital Services (Music)

It was only in Phase 3 that we have seen this phenomenon and it will be interesting to see if the move from office-based premises to home endures over time or whether more businesses start-up as a home-based incubator and move to office premises.

5.2.1   Reliability of Service

In Phase 2, we found that SMEs equate faster speeds and being able to achieve tasks such as sending large files quickly and easily as the result of having a more "reliable" connection. That is, when things ran smoothly the connection was considered to be reliable but when SMEs struggle to achieve tasks they judge their connection to be unreliable. SMEs operate in an increasingly connected world where new expectations are put upon them to respond in an agile and efficient manner. Key to the ability to achieve this was confidence in the reliability of fibre connectivity. In Phase 2, participants were delighted with what they described as a new-found reliability with SFBB, but in Phase 3 they were less enthusiastic about this aspect.

A minority of participants had no complaints whatsoever about reliability of service but for those who did, those complaints centred on the perception that their service was dropping out and some tasks that could be achieved easily in one day, took longer on another:

> You know, I was getting 85 when I was first on it, and it's dropping, but I assume it's probably because more people in the area are joining up to it... So that probably is going to affect it, but it's still pretty damn quick. I think it's the consistency, you know, one day I'll sit there going "Right, I'm going to do this," and it, it's done before I can think about it almost. Another day it's going to be 15 minutes, you know? Doing something, downloading a great big file or something, and yeah, why does the same thing take, you know, a few seconds yesterday? Digital Services

This perception was reinforced by those participants whose businesses offered IT support or digital services to other SMEs who cited slow speeds and inconsistent service as the most common problem reported by their customer base:

> Speed, I guess, that's probably the most common problem, it's not running as fast. A lot of people feel that the service isn't so reliable as it was. Digital Services

Participants who experienced fluctuations in their service described this as a source of frustration:

> We have outages in Truro all the time. I say outages but you wouldn't necessarily notice it unless you were actually on the Internet and suddenly you can't get onto a site. You have to come out, go back in and suddenly you can get back in again – and it's not just me because I work above a solicitor's office and they have exactly the same problems. Financial Services

It was possible that SME perceptions have changed because their expectations of what they can achieve through fibre connectivity have risen and the way they use the Internet has changed as more was accomplished online. SMEs need to embrace an "always on," increasingly connected world and this has altered their own and their clients' expectations and business practices:

> It's evolved a lot more in that, tools and software and packages etc., it's all online-based now. When I was an engineer with the local authority, when I first started I had a silver briefcase full of disks. If you turn up at a client's office or house now, it doesn't matter, they've got a printer and you say, "Have you got the disks for it?" And if they haven't, fine, you go online, go the manufacturer, and it might be a 300 Mb file, but within two or three minutes it's down and you can install it.... Digital Services

When questioned about whether perceived fluctuations in reliability hampered work activities, generally the answer was "no" – at present, although some described devising workarounds to accommodate difficulties:

> It's mainly uploading, because we tend to work offline on clients' files... and go back online and so we don't sync all the time, because if you did that then all your computers would run slow, so we tend to work offline and then synch it and send it back up and pull it back and down that way. It's the upload speeds, it's adequate but it could be faster. Financial Services

Not everyone was unhappy about SFBB services not being as reliable as they would like; one participant who ran a pub said that this was good for business:

> Funnily enough, when you say about what happens when the broadband goes down... I'm having the reverse of that. A lot of my clients, people that come in

to the pub, customers, they're all on outlying farms and a lot of them run farming type businesses, self-employed plumbers, electricians, plasterers and they all need the broadband to do quotes and things. When theirs goes down, which happens a lot in the rural areas . . . they come and sit in the pub and use mine now, so I'm, if you like my business is gaining. . . . Leisure and Tourism

Even though many participants said that their SFBB was not as reliable as they would like, they also said it was still a vast improvement over regular broadband provision.

5.2.2   Consistency of Service

Issues concerning reliability and consistency of service were complex and interlinked at several levels with problems concerning speed and interruptions to service. Participants complained that SFBB was not as consistent a service as they would like it to be. Even though glitches may only last for a few minutes, participants said that this has an impact on their business. Others were convinced that services were being throttled by Internet Service Providers (ISPs):

It's great, you know, it's revolutionary really. My only concern is that occasionally it gets throttled and it stops for, say, three to four minutes, not very often, but it does do that. Part of my business has been providing broadcast codex using an ISDN line for point to point broadcast use, and those are normally 99% reliable, perhaps even better, but the problem is, we could start doing it via the broadband, but if it's going to be broken down at a moment's notice, if it happens to be the vital moment when you want to use it, it's no good. It will appear to then reboot itself, say, five minutes later and then it's fine again for six months, well, it's fine again for three months anyway, but you just never know when it's going to happen and it's so critical. Broadcast Services

In the course of the discussions, many issues regarding reliability and consistency of service focused on geographical location in the county and variations in quality. Some participants described their service as having become "sporadic":

It's met with expectations but it's too sporadic. There are peaks and troughs, you know? e-Commerce Website Development

The coverage isn't just sporadic in terms of localities, I find it's sporadic during the day, the speeds vary. Architect

Not everyone had experienced problems and many reported that their SFBB service was stable and reliable but it does highlight the issue of SFBB services not being consistent across the region and how reliant they can be upon the underlying infrastructure:

> I think it's been very stable, which is a good thing. Pretty much, I think we've had it go down once, which is great. Compared to copper, you know, the stability is certainly there. Artist

Technological constraints impact on the quality of the service that can be delivered to particular premises and in some areas this was more common than in others. Although participants have complaints about the consistency of service, generally these problems are not impacting on the running of business effectively to any significant degree at present.

5.2.3   Current Bandwidth Consumption

Participants agreed that demands on communication technology were increasing and that SFBB was helping them to meet those demands:

> Files are getting bigger and bigger, but Superfast obviously helped that immensely. I think it's helped the clients send files using FTP sites to transfer files and Dropbox and things like that, it makes working life a lot easier. Then it's opening up the doors to other clients around the world too, around the country, you know? It's a lot easier to communicate.... Artist

Upload speeds have become increasingly significant in running a business; the way our SME population used their broadband connection has evolved and the increased upload capability of fibre connectivity was a significant driver for choosing SFBB in Phase 2. For the majority of SMEs, upload speed was now as important as download speed and this was not just confined to those business sectors that are traditionally bandwidth hungry:

> The upstream speed is the defining factor for us because it depends how many video calls we can make at any one time. It determines how good the quality of the calls can be, so the downstream speed is much less relevant. Digital Services

It was brilliant when we first got it but I need more upload...definitely. Landscape and Garden Design

More and more businesses were turning to Cloud services and there was a growing need to be able to quickly upload increasingly large documents, and to be able to retrieve them with the same speed efficiency. Participants said that current upload and download speeds, whilst useable currently, are not likely to be adequate in the near future:

We're on the edge, it's just about OK. Business Services

It's all promoted on the download speed; 30 MB, 40 MB whatever...but I need better upload speeds. Customers are doing a video on their iPhone, or whatever it may be and then they are uploading that to Facebook, so you know...we need more upload, definitely. Tourism and Hospitality

When questioned about bandwidth consumption, participants invariably cited increasing file sizes, media hungry applications and streaming as the main sources:

It's streaming, an awful lot of people streaming all the time. There's quite a lot that want to do the odd Google search and check their email, but a lot of them now are streaming different things, which takes up most of my bandwidth. Tourism and Hospitality

This led to a wider discussion concerning the disparity between upload and download speeds and as in Phase 1 of our research, we heard SMEs voicing a requirement for a symmetrical service. This was interesting because whilst we heard many requests for a symmetrical service in Phase 1, this had all but disappeared in Phase 2 when participants said that fibre connectivity was fast enough for them to accomplish all that they needed. It would appear that SMEs quickly learn to exploit fibre capability and this, in combination with increasing file sizes, drives their requirement, particularly with regard to increased upload capability:

We do need it as a utility and we do need to synchronise both up and down, absolutely. I'm getting about 75 down and 15 to 18 up but it would be nicer if it was symmetrical. Digital Services

There was evidence that a desire for a symmetrical service was sector dependant but again, the focus was on upload speeds and an increase in capacity may see this requirement disappear:

> I'm getting about the same but I could do with more upload speed. Just a higher speed up would help. Most of the time it's alright, when I've got to send multi-tracks...because most of the time I am downloading multi-tracks which are gigabytes and then I am just sending back the mixes which are 100 megabytes instead. So most of the time if I want to send multi-tracks to other people, then I just have to sit and wait. Most of the time it is alright the way it is. Digital Services (music)

For some sectors upload speeds are not an issue:

> For our business it is not a major issue, if I want to update our website I just set it going and I walk away and do something else while it is doing that and the fact that it has a 1meg upload speed, that doesn't really affect me that much. Farming and Tourism

It was interesting to note that those who had access to greater bandwidth and those on FTTP showed little enthusiasm for a symmetrical service other than the fact that "it would be nice" which supports the notion that this requirement only appears when SMEs are struggling to accomplish tasks online and disappears when their service was "fast enough:"

> It would be nice to have the choice, but I have to say I think a lot of it is academic. I mean what's the difference between say in taking 30 seconds and 40 seconds, or 20 seconds? Digital Services

> "We're past that, it was only relevant when we were only getting 1 or 2 MB upload." Web-based Services

It was also interesting to note that when participants were pressed further with regards to upload and download speeds, they reverted to telling us that reliability and confidence in the service, coupled with excellent customer service are most important. Aspirations focused on the importance of stability and speed and participants said it was difficult to choose one over the other:

It's got to be both really, you need speed and you need reliability, the service has to be stable. Hospitality and Tourism

The problems that participants raised indicate just how much their use of the Internet has changed; they now depend more heavily on connectivity to operate their businesses effectively than ever before and this strongly influences their expectations and aspirations. It was difficult to unpack whether the desire for a symmetrical service simply masks a desire for greater upload capacity more generally, or whether for some, there was a genuine requirement for equivalent upload and download capacity.

5.3 Future Proofing and Bandwidth Consumption

Regardless of whether participants said they needed a symmetrical service, all were convinced that bandwidth requirements were growing and that this was technology driven – as more becomes possible, needs grow:

> I'm hoping that the speeds increase, or we're going to have to look at sort of increasing it somehow, because, especially with the uploading, because we're going to have lots of job sheets, or technical data flying back, so we're going to have an issue there, so I hope it speeds up. We need it to improve significantly to be able to continue offering that service to our customers. Business Services

Many participants described themselves as being "on the edge" with regard to their bandwidth requirements, and when questioned about whether SFBB offered a future proof solution for businesses in the region they said that the current service was adequate, but must be improved to meet future needs:

> I think that certainly from my perspective, and I suspect it's probably shared around the group, one of the most important things about the Superfast Broadband is that it gives me the confidence to be able to take things forward, you know? Because I know that I'm going to be able to do the work when I need to be able to do. As things get more difficult, that confidence will begin to tail off. Therefore you will want more to be provided, because as more and more people are using it, as the infrastructure is not renewed and with some of the infrastructure issues, your confidence will start to fall. That would be a very big problem as far as I'm

concerned...because I will not be able to deliver that which my clients expect me to deliver. Digital Services

Some participants pointed to an increasing use of Cloud services and told us that while their service was "good enough – for now" it was unlikely to be so in the future unless there are improvements in bandwidth capacity:

> It needs to be future proof...and also to be ready for the next influx of Cloud-based software. I have a client and they've got like 17 machines all accessing an Internet-based database...it's OK now but...the more businesses go onto Cloud-based software, the more the Internet speed is going to be paramount. Digital Services

As many participants ran their business from home when asked about the largest source of bandwidth consumption they responded with "Teenagers!" and the ways in which domestic consumption was expanding:

> My kids! I think it is the kids streaming YouTube that uses more bandwidth than anything else; in fact I think I am considering limiting their bandwidth through my switch. The other month it was over 100 gig and that is just...we are not streaming music around the world and all the rest of it, this is just kids watching it and holiday makers, I think that is where it's coming from, it's watching things on the Internet. Farming and Tourism

Broadband use has been growing steadily over the last 10 years and is likely to continue to do so as more applications are developed and become available online:

> I don't think I am future proofed, I think people's needs will increase but they do keep saying, here's a new technology, they are trying new things out and hopefully we've got a decent line now and that may be able to keep up with future advances. Digital Services

When asked about current bandwidth consumption and future needs, some participants said that current fibre provision had been adequate to accomplish current business needs but this was not the case any longer. However, when pressed further we found that this was not because their bandwidth needs had changed, it was because they perceived their service to be slower that it had been when they first signed up:

I would say mine isn't fast enough at the moment...because it's slowed down. Digital Services

Those participants who experienced the slowest speeds also predicted that that they would need more bandwidth to accommodate their business needs in the coming 2–5 years:

I don't think it will be fast enough. I'm realising that some people have got double the upload speeds that we have, and although we've achieved a great deal since we've had it – we've started to expand with our video stuff overseas for example, but if we had 100% more upload speed I'm sure that would make what we do even more efficient. If we do more elaborate productions, or we actually start helping other people to produce some of their stuff, it will reach a point where it's not good enough. We started the conversation saying how well it all goes, but we need to make sure that everything else is switched off. So all our mobile phones, everything, so that the upload speed is not diluted by any other device in the house, so our teenage sons have to actually power down lap-tops, everything, because we have to make sure that all of the bandwidth is ours. But if we had double, maybe that wouldn't be such a problem. Digital Services

In response to the question "how much is enough?" participants cited upload speeds and consistency as being most important once again:

If someone's getting 18 MB per second upload speed, then I'd like that, because it's double what we're getting and I can see that that would really make a difference to us. The download speeds I'm not so fussed about, because you know, 38 MB per second, whatever I'm downloading, if the kids are downloading a movie, or I'm downloading a giant file, it's going to come down really quickly anyway. It's the upload speed that's important.... Digital Services

It's consistency that's important actually. IT Services

Participants also voiced a strong desire for fibre connectivity to be standardised in the future which ties in with participant issues about what exactly constitutes "Superfast":

The Internet is going to be the backbone of the economy in this country because we are so service-led. There really needs to be a standardisation of Superfast performance. Just suppose one of you decided for whatever reason to move from where you are to another part of Cornwall. You got used to 65 MB...And suddenly you move down to me and you're down to 10...there should be standardisation of performance, throughout the county. Financial Services

Clearly, bandwidth consumption is set to grow and SMEs were concerned that current broadband provision will not meet their needs in the next 2–5 years. This was a complex issue bound up with the variability in the different levels of service available in different areas across the region – those with the poorest level of service showed the strongest concerns, as did those with the most bandwidth-hungry businesses. There was a strong desire amongst participants to feel that they are future proofed and many are concerned at the increasingly fast pace of domestic consumption that may impact on their ability to run their businesses as effectively as they would like. Again, this was an issue that we heard in Phase 1 of our research and whilst we have not come full circle, SMEs fear that we might. With regard to future proofing participants told us that speed, reliability and consistency of service were still top of their wish list and that they will require greater bandwidth provision very soon in order to maintain their current levels of productivity.

5.4   BENEFITS REALISATION AND INNOVATION

In Phase 2 we found that having experienced SFBB, the value it provides quickly becomes deeply embedded in SMEs daily work practices and processes through benefits realisation and as a result, dependence on connectivity increases. Inevitably, the benefits and opportunities that SFBB affords overlap and in many cases are interdependent, and in Phase 3 we found that SFBB has maintained a pivotal role in delivering value through new-found efficiencies, savings, improved business processes and innovation:

I think for us it's improved the way we were already using the Internet – it's taken a few systems which were barely usable, and made them incredible reliable. One of the key things we use it for is a beaconing connection between point to point, between various offices. With an old ADSL connection it dropped quite frequently, it was very, very slow, especially with the high encryption rate, and we use a lot of intensive database software, which required a very stable connection, which was just unusable. So having an incredibly stable, high speed connection has made that, you know, a very usable part of the business. It's made a fantastic difference. Digital Services and Wine Merchant

In Phase 3, it was interesting to note that when describing the myriad benefits of fibre connectivity, participants made the distinction between availability of fibre and the technological/Internet developments that are available to them as a result. Hence, they perceive SFBB as an enabling technology that makes accessing the Internet/applications and the advantages that affords, much easier and more effective. Dial up, and to a lesser extent ADSL technology, were perceived as a necessary but inconvenient barrier to access, whereas fibre connectivity provides a far more seamless experience that renders the technology of delivery all but invisible:

What SFBB enables... it makes technology transparent I think, it's the systems that the Superfast broadband has allowed us to use that's allowed us to change how we do things... not the Superfast if you see what I mean. Architect

To be able to do all that... it's not Superfast itself... it's the Internet itself as opposed to.... Digital Services

In Phase 2, not only had participants quickly become accustomed to faster speeds and greater bandwidth capacity but they also reported having become increasingly reliant on better connectivity to run their businesses effectively. This far exceeded their reliance on previous broadband provision because it enables them to do so much more, and to work in new and different ways that exploit the advantage of greater speeds and bandwidth capacity. In Phase 3, this dependency has grown alongside even greater benefit realisation and innovation.

5.4.1   Innovation and Operating Differently

One of the greatest benefits of fibre connectivity for SMEs was that it enables businesses to operate differently and this fosters innovations that would not have been possible before. We found evidence of different ways of working in Phase 2, but in Phase 3 participants were able to report many more areas of business impact after devising new ways to exploit their connectivity. For some it had opened up global markets and new ways of delivering their services:

> I'm a professional violinist and a composer and with Google Plus you can use this tool called "Hangouts on Air" . . . it just means that you can broadcast live globally, and as a musician I've been having my own show and broadcasting live music concerts all over the world, and we are the first people in the UK to achieve this, which is quite incredible . . . So without Superfast we wouldn't have been able to do that. Digital Services

SFBB was also changing the way services are delivered in house:

> We decided to do an online version of our meetings, at two o'clock, just after lunchtime on a Wednesday once a month and that's worked really well because we have about eight or nine people meet through the camera. We made the last one public, which meant other people outside of the group could watch and comment on what we were talking about. That went quite well. Digital Services

Several participants described being able to broaden the scope of what they are able to offer to clients that far exceeded their initial expectations of SFBB:

> For us, being able to host servers for clients is something that is amazing, whilst you don't have a guaranteed service level agreement we've got servers in a London data centre that's got a resilient connection and diesel generator backups, that sort of thing, and we have got servers in our office in Cornwall. They are each pinged sort of every five minutes to check their up time. The one in Cornwall has got 100% in the last year, whereas the ones in the data centre tend to be 98% or so. To have something that we can rely on that well is . . . phenomenal, and it's secure as well. Digital Services and Wine Merchant

Participants are also starting to exploit new markets:

> I must admit it's opened up a new sort of market for us really with hosted telephone systems and these trunk lines over broadband. Telecommunications

In Phase 2 we uncovered the *Virtuous Circle of Connectivity* through a chain of interdependent benefits of SFBB that have become so important to SMEs that they have become far more reliant on fibre connectivity than they ever were on regular broadband. As SME reliance on SFBB benefits grows, this increases and reinforces the value, new dependencies are forged and a new set of values and benefits emerge that are used to even greater effect. This is certainly still in evidence, and dependency on SFBB has grown further in Phase 3 such that SMEs told us they could not consider operating their business without it:

If you are living in Cornwall then I can't believe how you can not have it now really, because of the difference it's made. Web Developer

You can't really go into an online business without it. You'd be on the back step to anyone else around you, even your customers; you can't really deliver, add value, or give them the service that they would expect without it. e-Commerce

SFBB was not just an improved way of working; it was a different way of working. SFBB was what makes the web work, it makes the mechanics of delivery transparent and the opportunities it affords are bounded only by the imagination of its users to operate in different ways and develop new innovations.

5.4.2   Speed and Efficiency Gains

The most obvious benefit of SFBB for SMEs was in speed and efficiency gains and in Phase 2 these benefits were the most readily articulated; only those SMEs who were more bandwidth dependent identified additional benefits over and above increased speed. Speed and efficiency gains are important factors that impact on business productivity and these are still in evidence in Phase 3:

The delivery aspect of video – it used to be a quarter to half a working day and now it's actually quicker to upload and deliver the video than it is to export it out of the editing software. The property world doesn't like to innovate, so the technology was always a stumbling block and one of the many excuses...so we can get rid of that issue. Now we can basically turn around video tours, like news gatherings, in 48 hours. Property Services

However, in Phase 3, SMEs described a much wider range of benefits that they readily articulated in terms of the difference fibre connectivity has made to their business. In the course of discussions, it became apparent that far more participants are uncovering benefits that make working practices not just quantitatively better (i.e. faster), but qualitatively better in terms of what can be accomplished:

I'm just starting up a new business in craft and producing all sorts of things, but I do a lot of research and finding products, bits and pieces that I need and really trying to get the best prices, and it's fantastic to be able to do it with Superfast. It's made a heck of a difference; I don't spend half as much time looking. Creative Design

Participants also told us about being able to increase their productivity as a result of better connectivity:

It's definitely increased our productivity; one of our sales managers is now able to work out in the field with the software that we run directly to the epos system which means that he doesn't have to travel back and forth to the shop quite so much. Digital Services and Wine Merchant

And SFBB was still helping SMEs to accomplish tasks that were previously difficult and time consuming to achieve:

I used to hate doing VAT returns and dealing with the bank and all these other things. Now of course it's dead easy. I mean it is just so convenient. My company has a number of sort of associate consultants and so I have to make sure they get paid at the end of the week, because they invoice weekly, and you know, it's dead easy, no problems at all. I can sit there, do it on a Saturday or a Sunday and they've got money in their account on the Monday. Business Services

In Phase 3, very few participants felt that the advantages of SFBB were limited to operating more quickly and most were able to describe a much wider range of benefits.

5.4.3   Better Access to Worldwide Markets

Locating and winning new customers was vital to the survival and future growth of businesses in the region. Participants were keen to describe the way in which they have exploited fibre connectivity to open up new access to worldwide markets and were enthusiastic about the opportunities this provides for collaboration and business growth:

Our aspirations for what we could use Superfast for, it's been beyond what we could have hoped for really, you know? Because we've got clients now in parts of the world we just couldn't have talked to, and I think because of the way that social media and the Internet is moving towards more like relation-ship marketing and transparency and people being authentic and being yourself, if you can actually suddenly appear on someone's screen and you start talking to them in real time, people get to know you so much faster, and you make a decision whether you are going to do business with that person on a much more efficient basis than emailing them, or writing to them, or whatever. Management Consultancy

Even where participants had not yet brought their ideas to fruition, they were enthused about the opportunity:

I'd like to get more into the export side, that's what I'm aiming for. So if this new website comes along…I get a lot of export enquiries from customers who come through the eBay shop. So they'll see the item on there, and they'll contact me off eBay and I'm hoping that they can do it through the website instead of through eBay, which will be nicer. I get a lot of repeat business from eBay, but I would like to get videos and things up so they can actually see me, you know? And then they get to know me better, so that would be quite good. Retail

Participants also talked about being able to exploit access to global resources both in terms of information and in accessing expertise from others:

The fact that you can just reach out and get help on a global basis, you know? It's just fantastic. Without Superfast it would not have been possible. Digital Services

It was interesting to note that access to SFBB has also had the reverse effect in that businesses that could previously only offer services outside of the region can now serve the local population too:

The services that we only ever offered up-country before, we can now offer locally, which is nice, you know? We were only ever doing business in London and around London when we were selling just the video-conferencing hardware, because nobody down here wanted to spend that money, not at that cost. And all of a sudden, the services we can offer are low cost and they're available to any small business down this way that just was not possible before Superfast came along, so it's been an absolute boon for us. Digital Services

Rural businesses suffer from remoteness from extended markets but fibre connectivity offers new-found access to global markets that is continuing to promote business growth and enables SMEs to create new revenue streams.

5.5 BROADENING THE CUSTOMER BASE

We found increasing evidence of participants accessing a broader customer base as a result of fibre connectivity in Phase 3:

> I can now support clients abroad, which I couldn't really do before. Since Superfast arrived I can have reliable conference calls. I mean beforehand, before we got Superfast suddenly the conference call would come to an end. It would depend upon the weather, either at my end, or his end or, you know what the day of the week was, but now you can do it reliably. I can accept work from the United States or from Europe or whatever and have a good chance of being able to deliver on it. Business Services

Greater connectivity was providing SMEs with greater confidence, enabling them to broaden their customer base within the UK and further afield and this was supporting business growth in the region.

5.5.1   Increased Use of Cloud Services

SMEs are keen to access new and affordable technology and for many this was seen as one of the tipping points for business success. Without adequate bandwidth use of Cloud services was severely curtailed but fibre connectivity makes this possible and participants were quick to take-up the opportunity to exploit the benefits. While we had seen a take-up of Cloud services in Phase 2, their use was very much mainstreamed in our Phase 3 focus groups:

> Superfast has finally made the Cloud a reality I think from both a reliability perspective and a performance perspective. Marketing

Innovations in Cloud technology offer a fundamentally different way for SMEs to harness computational power, storage capacity and services, and SFBB acts as a catalyst that provokes change in working practices as more possibilities are opened up through improved bandwidth capacity. In combination, Cloud services and SFBB provide SMEs with a new set of very powerful tools and many felt these are fundamental to running a business effectively:

> We have an office that we built into our extended home and we've had Superfast since its inception, we're off the Devoran exchange, which was one of the first that was connected. Like other businesses everything now is Internet-based and we are as well. We keep all our drawings in the Cloud. We have all our software, not in the Cloud, but it's going that way, so yeah, that's what we do, the normal stuff, but we aren't so Internet-based that we need a server as such . . . but we do have very important communication links, again, with the Cloud where we are sharing stuff with clients so they can see what we are doing for them, making comment on drawings and what have you. Architect

> One of the things that's happened over the last 12 months is using Cloud computing . . . and that is a big issue with whatever connection speeds you've got by virtue of the fact that everything is going that way, even your software upgrades and everything is coming from the Cloud now. e-Commerce Web Site Development

Participants described how use of Cloud services has meant they can cut their IT expenditure:

> The surprising thing that I've managed to achieve, which I've always wanted to achieve, is that it's allowed me to go serverless. I've got rid of all my servers. I now, all of my applications now run in the Cloud, all my storage of everything is done in the Cloud, all I do is replicate stuff back to a NAS network, attached storage box, in my premises. I don't have to have three or four servers doing all this stuff. I don't have to think about keeping them going now. Marine Technologies

Participants were also appreciative of the value add and peace of mind of automatic backups via the Cloud:

> I've got a client . . . I hold a back-up for them on my network. So every night a copy of their data streams into my server, and that seems a lot better. I certainly wouldn't like to do it on normal broadband really, I reckon that would struggle. Digital Services

> It was our accountant that came over and said, "Well, what if you have a fire? You're going to lose everything. There's no point backing it up on something you keep in the office." So it all goes to the Cloud now. . . . Financial Services

Use of Cloud services also provides SMEs with different ways of working that mean they can share information with clients and offer greater transparency to their customers:

> These days... the way it's going is a lot of people demand access to certain packages that you use so that they can see what's happening with all their investments and things like that and now I can do that on the Cloud. Financial Services

> VoIP gives us the opportunity now to integrate our Cloud services into voice services, so where we want CTI telephony integration and that sort of thing, it now gives us the ability because it's all in the Cloud to actually take that a stage further forward as well. Yeah, it allows us to take services outside of County. I think one of the big things is with Superfast, it finally makes Cloud-based applications, Cloud-based ERP systems a reality, whereas on ADSL it really wasn't fast enough, but we're now finding we can put Cloud-based ERP systems on a server and it's as fast as on premise. So now... where we could only provide ERP in Cornwall we can now look at taking that outside of County, so hopefully it gives us the opportunity to extend our market place much more. From a sales perspective it's good for us. Marketing

Participants spoke of how using Cloud services has enabled them to be more efficient and better serve their customers:

> With the Cloud side of it, it's ideal because now with the Cloud software from doing their accounts, they've got direct feeds, their bank accounts download information every night and everything else, but we can actually go on and help them as we can look at it remotely with them and help them out if they've got a query or anything else. Again, we don't have to catch up with them December, January to sign bits of paper; they can do that electronically.... Business Services

> We do that too, we are already using Cloud software for our clients' accounts systems, they are done in the Cloud, so it's all backed up and everything else, and we can even send your tax return in a secure area, you can actually read it, sign it off electronically and send that back again, so it's working really well. Business Services

Using collaborative tools via Cloud services was also high on the agenda and participants found this time efficient and reliable:

Collaboration is another issue that's come on, but all these things you learn as you go along and it dawns on you that they are available. I mean a lot of the work we do, if I've got a structural engineer, he can access the drawing that I've been working on and he can work on it. That is tremendous and it stays in the same place, and it updates and says, "So and so's done this work on it." So that's another brilliant advantage of the Internet. Well, I suppose it's Cloud-based again, but all these things that happen.... Architect

Participants also described how access to Cloud services has been transformational for business, enabling the development of new processes to facilitate greater effectiveness and promote efficiency:

It's transforming the way that we run our business because we're predominantly out servicing. We've got 5,000 Cornish customers and we service fire alarms, fire extinguishers and all that type of stuff. So what we are doing is designing a bit of software, we're currently beta testing it. It's early days yet, but we're hoping to roll it out across our 15 engineers shortly. We've basically got it on a tablet which connects to a CRM system in the Cloud and an engineer will be using it on tablet, filling it all in there and then when the job is done, clicks it's done and emails through to the customer with the invoice, sends them the certificate, worksheet, the whole lot and updates the CRM system as well. It's given a better customer experience, it's more sustainable, it's a lot faster, you know, with the CRM system where all the dockets are stored online, so if you need a copy invoice, or pay an invoice, it can all be done online. You know, it's moving along with the times, it's making it greener, faster and the customers like it. Business Services

SMEs were becoming increasingly reliant on Cloud services and are appreciative of the reliability of services like Dropbox and the confidence this engenders in delivery:

I just drag into Dropbox and forget about it, and it will be there, not possibly there or maybe there – it'll be there. IT Services

In order to take full advantage of Cloud services, SMEs again highlighted the need for adequate upload and download capacity:

Download speed is not too much of a problem, upload speed it what concerns us more because we were uploading this afternoon and I think we uploaded about 17 Gb of stuff back up to the Cloud but it went very quickly because our upload speed is upwards of 30 Mb, it took 20 minutes... and I upload a big database every now and then that goes up in a few seconds, so that's fine. Financial Services

For those on the move, this was particularly important as bandwidth capacity may not be sufficient at the locations they are likely to visit, not just in Cornwall but elsewhere, and this was hampering more widespread use in some cases:

I don't use it because I've found all my files are so huge, either InDesign or Photoshop or whatever. I just back it up, you know, to other hard drives. I just find that's a lot more time saved, rather than trying to download something, and especially if I travel and I want to take my lap-top, I'll take a little portable hard drive. I've thought, well do I just put it on the Cloud, but then depending where I am, I don't know what the broadband is going to be like, and if I want to change a Photoshop file and it's 100 MB file, I'm going to have to rely on downloading it and I don't know what speed that will be, so I can't rely on it at the moment. Web Development

Speed of retrieval due to slow download speeds was an issue for some and this influenced decisions about whether or not to use Cloud storage:

I think it is useful for synchronising documents and stuff like that but for big files, I think I would keep them local because of retrieval; you need to have them back quick. Digital Services (IT Support)

Amongst those participants using Cloud services for backup and storage there was still a degree of ignorance about wider business benefits:

I still think sometimes, "Oh, I don't use anything in the Cloud," but actually I probably do, because I've been using Apple Macs since '84, I'm one of those original Mac users. What I did find very interesting is that my iPhone, my wife's iPhone and her iPad, her lap-top, my two desktops, all know what each other is doing, everything, all the time, and that again is a Cloud system. Management Consultancy

However, in the course of discussions it became apparent that there was still poor understanding of Cloud hosting amongst some SMEs with regard to where their data were located:

> Could be anywhere . . . God knows where it is . . . It could be in Iceland as far as I know. Architect

> You have different types of Cloud . . . You have your . . . what people think of the Cloud is in America somewhere. . . . Tourism and Hospitality

And a minority were delaying adoption due to scepticism and concerns about security:

> It's another one of those things where everyone says it's wonderful and then somebody comes up with all these disadvantages about it not being secure, or you can't get stuff back . . . and all this. It's another thing I will keep thinking about, I'll wait and see what the outcome is you know, I think that it is more . . . supposedly its secured but every so often something pops up saying, "No, it's not," it makes you wait a little while I think. . . . Hospitality and Tourism

Although such doubts were countered by discussion from others:

> I wanted to keep it in-house because it's much quicker to retrieve but nonetheless, I was over-ruled. I am not particularly worried about security and certainly, if you are protected from fire or theft it is much better to be in a humungous data centre that is secure that way. If we are talking about data transfer security then you know that is as much of a threat as when you have got it in house, if you get a virus or anything else. We did have a few people that work out of the office in different locations and for them to be able to pull it off whenever they want, is better. Digital Services and Wine Merchant

Some had adopted a "belt and braces" approach to ensure access and security:

> I'm not saying it isn't secure, I just don't like the fact that someone else has got my database somewhere else and at some time they can pull the plug and I can't get at it. I'm backed up on the Cloud, but I've got everything on my server as well, because it's there and it's mine and I can get at it when I want it. Financial Services

As noted above, those who had not adopted Cloud services were in a minority and most of these were still in the process of considering this as an option:

> I am considering it, I haven't done it yet but I have got such a massive archive. . . . Digital Services (music)

> I'm not sold, so I don't do anything with Cloud, other than what's done with whatever I'm using. I don't actually do it myself, but then we're not in the sort of business that we really need to. . . . Historical Research

In facilitating the use of Cloud services, SFBB offers SMEs the opportunity to revolutionise the way they work and compete far more effectively with their larger rivals. Cloud services offer SMEs the opportunity to reduce their IT expenditure and this provides flexibility and frees up funds that can be directed towards other aspects of the business. The ease, convenience and cost savings Cloud services provide are set to play an increasingly important role in the evolution of SME IT operations. In Phase 3, after longer experience of using SFBB, increased use of Cloud services was proving transformative for business and emerging as a major disruptive force.

5.5.2   Business Creation and Retention in Cornwall

In response to questions regarding whether fibre access had enabled businesses to remain located in Cornwall, Phase 3 participants were very positive and several said that they had been considering relocating out of the county before the introduction of fibre:

> Without Superfast we wouldn't have stayed in Cornwall, well we couldn't I mean, but now. . . . Digital Services (Music)

> I would have been looking at moving up country without the Superfast, we couldn't have grown the business the way we want to without it. Financial Services

One participant had relocated from London to Cornwall and described how fibre connectivity had enabled him to retain London customers:

It's meant that I can bring work with me when I moved down to Cornwall from London that I expected that I would lose, but because I can now shift large files very quickly, there can be a program shot in the studio and they can send me all the audio files and I can put them together and get them back quite quickly. So I didn't lose that work which actually was quite valuable. There's a couple of guys in the broadcast field I know, both of them post production houses in Soho, incredibly busy, talented guys, upped sticks, and moved the family down to Cornwall because of Superfast, Broadcast Services

Others spoke of fibre connectivity protecting existing jobs in Cornwall and fostering business growth resulting in job creation opportunities both now and in the future:

We've expanded and I guess we've expanded on the back of broadband. I don't think we would have expanded as much, and every time you take people on I suppose you're providing job security for the ones that are there as well. I mean it's always difficult to say isn't it? Whether our expansion is because of superfast broadband or whether we would have expanded anyway – we like to think we would have done anyway but, you know. . . . Management Consultancy

Over the last two years we have increased the number of people working, and because of that we did upgrade our web designer. Leisure and Tourism

In discussions regarding job creation as a result of SFBB the situation was more complex than might be expected. We did find instances of business growth and resultant job creation in Phase 3:

I'd quite like to take on an e-commerce assistant, because I spend so much time on the eBay and the website that I sometimes forget about my Cornish customers. I can't get to enough of them, so. . . . Retail

However, as in Phase 2, many participants reported how better connectivity enabled them to collaborate with those who have the expertise they need outside of the county, and often outside of the UK, on short-term contracts. Hence, there was growing evidence of employment changes and working differently as a direct result of SFBB. Whilst there was evidence of job creation, it may not be easily traceable and may not be confined to Cornwall, or even the UK:

We collaborate with a much wider group now, in Spain, Germany and France, we've even got someone in the States...just now and then we call on them to do something for us...short term contracts and that sort of thing. Digital Services

SFBB was widely available in the region but was not available everywhere due to technological constraints but it has become so important to business that some SMEs described giving up business premises where SFBB was not available, and working from home instead where it was:

During those two years when they were promising it was coming, next week, next week, next week – for two years...unbelievable...I was going to move, I couldn't do what I was trying to do, it was holding me back. When you were down in the Sawmills it was a nightmare with ISDN lines, down at the Sawmills in Fowey. It's the same now, you still can't get any bandwidth, it's in the middle of nowhere and the telephone lines come all the way from Fowey all the way to Castle Dor, all the way down to Golant and all the way back. It's all straight lines to lay the cables, but it's ridiculous and it is just impossible, it was never going to happen...I am running my business from my house now, 'cause I can get it there. Digital Services (Music)

In this context, it was interesting to note that whilst some participants talked about giving up business premises because SFBB was not available but they could get access from home, others reported giving up their business premises because they are now more productive and no longer need business premises:

I have tried the shop and the offices and stuff, but I have sort of come back a bit and I have made that move already, I will probably be a bit busier but...I can be home-based now, I don't need to go back out there again really. Digital Services (IT Support)

It was also interesting to note that some participants found it valuable to be able to hide the fact that they are operating from Cornwall because of perceived negative perceptions about their ability to deliver:

The other beauty of it is that if you've got a website and it's a good website, people don't look necessarily where you are, and you can appear to be much bigger than you are. It's influencing perceptions. As long as you give the service people don't worry...and they don't necessarily look that you're in Cornwall . . . Most of our clients aren't local to us. And with some of them, it will be two or three conversations down the line before they say, "Oh, where is it that you're based?" And you tell them "Cornwall, is that a problem?" and because you've already delivered they go, "No, that's fine." e-Commerce Website Development

Fibre connectivity was enabling SMEs to remain located in Cornwall, protecting existing jobs and was providing the infrastructure that helps overcome the region's peripheral location. There was evidence of job creation but employment patterns are changing with increased collaboration on short-term contracts both locally and farther afield. Many start-ups are operating from home and businesses are downsizing due to increased efficiencies with SFBB and swapping office-based working for home-based working.

5.5.3   Business Growth, New Business Opportunities and Diversification

Participants had already started to exploit the benefits of SFBB for business growth in Phase 2 and this has continued and was more widespread in Phase 3. Participants' enthusiasm for growing their businesses has increased as result of using SFBB and the new benefits and opportunities they have discovered as a result:

I just want to grow the company, you know? And get a couple more designers in, so I can take more of a director role and actually not so much hands-on. With Superfast I can think about taking more freelancers on around the country rather than just having them in the office. Web-based Services

Participants were excited about the possibilities of SFBB, even if they had not yet brought all their ideas to fruition:

I'm currently working on a project called The Diary of a Coastal Composer, which was inspired by, do you remember The Diary of the Edwardian Lady? Well this is more like a 21st century kind of multi-media thing. So I'm going to put it together like an iBook. My music is very inspired by the landscape, so it's going to be me . . . talking about where I've been . . . with photography, poems and artwork, video and music to go with it. So probably, it will be like a quarterly diary, so people will be able to buy it and watch on their Kindles and it will be multi-media. Professional Violinist and Composer

I export anyway, but only small amounts, but I'm hoping to get bigger contracts from that, and therefore uploading all the photographs and everything makes things easier. Retail

SFBB is supporting businesses in the region with strong growth ambitions and encouraging diversification and new opportunities for growth that would not otherwise be possible.

5.6   IMPACT ON CARBON FOOTPRINT

As we found in previous phases of the research, most participants showed little interest in green issues or carbon saving either in the course of running their businesses or as a result of fibre access, most were more concerned with the bottom line:

It's not an issue for anybody is it? It's all been proved to be absolutely rubbish. Digital Services (music)

I'm not worried about that. Digital Services (IT support)

Do you really think you can make an impact on this world, one little person? Yes, the big companies, they should be thinking about it, but I don't think the majority of us really think about it that much. Hospitality and Tourism

In Phase 3, there was some evidence of a reduction in carbon footprint through a reduced need to travel, working remotely, holding meetings over Skype, reduced use of paper in business processes and use of Cloud services. However, participants did not describe the benefits in terms of increasing their green credentials and carbon saving, these were implicit rather than explicit:

It's helped us not to travel as much, because I used to be going to London twice a month. Now I'm up once every six months. In that respect it's made a lot of difference. Time is money. Financial Services

With a lot of the companies we deal with, especially with things like pay runs and pensions and accountants and things like that, they can all access it remotely, so there's no paper flying everywhere. No paper getting lost, accurate information coming in. In some cases it's actually driven people's accountancy bills down, because the accountants have been able to access online and just draw the information off and then put it straight into their system... Saving time, saving money, yeah. Financial Services

A minority said that as they have expanded their customer base or grown their business as a result of SFBB, their carbon footprint has increased. This tended to be sector dependent according to the nature of the work involved and the necessity to be physically present in a particular location:

> Well I've actually increased in one respect on carbon footprint, it's because I'm bringing in clients from further away. Obviously I've had to go to France a couple of times to do photo-shoots and stuff and you can't do that without physically being there... but I wouldn't have been doing that job in the first place if it wasn't for the Superfast Broadband. But locally, it's decreased it a lot, because I'm just doing most of the things, you know, on the phone or on broadband. Web-based Services

As in Phase 2, participants were more interested in the bottom line than in increasing their green credentials. In Phase 3 we continued to find examples where a positive impact might occur at an individual level, but carbon saving benefits were not well articulated or acknowledged by participants.

5.6.1   Remote Working and Working from Home

In Phase 2, participants had started to realise the benefit of remote working but in Phase 3 this was much more prevalent:

> The remote working is something that we just couldn't do before, to have a decent quality call open all day, every day so that somebody's in the office with you. It makes a huge difference to them and to the office environment. That's something we couldn't have done before... Before he would be in a little office at home, you know, not feeling part of things, not picking up the vibe in the office. It's funny because this guy was not at all enthusiastic to start with, he thought he was being spied upon, but within a few weeks of having it he felt bereft if we were changing something and he couldn't be connected for the day. It's made a difference, an absolute profound difference... and we've saved a huge amount of money. Marketing

Participants also described how being able to work remotely saves time for their business and for their customers and adds value to the services they provide:

> I find a lot of my customers prefer the personal approach, but it certainly means that you can access remotely, if it's something you can't get to the customer's site to do, you say "Okay, well I'll remote in later when I'm in the office." And it does mean it's a lot easier to do that, and it also makes it easier to deal with further afield clients as well. You could be based in Cornwall and remotely servicing customers in London, Scotland, you know, whoever. Digital Services

Remote access also means that businesses can respond faster if an emergency arises, from wherever they are:

> If you've got something major that's happening while you're away, you're abroad or something, because of how the system is, you can be anywhere in the world, just plug in and see what's happening. Instead of fire-fighting you are being proactive by using the system and going forward like that, which you could never do before. Financial Services

Participants told us that SFBB makes location irrelevant; in Phase 3 we found that more SMEs are working from home (see also Section 6.9) and several have relocated from office premises to home working as a direct result of access to SFBB:

> You can actually operate your business wherever you want to. You can be on a farm in the middle of nowhere and you should be able to operate a business. As long as you're giving the right level of customer service and product, there's nothing stopping you. Digital Services

The increase in home-based businesses, remote working and the advent of SMEs swapping office premises for home-based working was growing in significance as a direct result of fibre connectivity. Access to fibre connectivity and advances in information communications technology (ICT) afford new ways of working and different ways of working and this makes running a business from home a compelling proposition, and one that was likely to grow.

5.7   THE EVER EXPANDING SKILLS GAP

In a fast-moving digital economy, the businesses most likely to succeed and grow are those with appropriately technically skilled staff. Digital literacy skills enable SMEs to exploit the knowledge and understanding they need to make full use of the opportunities presented by fibre connectivity. We can infer improved technical proficiency amongst participants in Phase 3 from an increased use of a range of applications and novel and broader use of services than were in evidence in Phase 2. However, as in Phase 2, in Phase 3 comments of those participants who worked in the computing industry or served the computing needs of fellow SMEs suggest that there was still a skills gap of which SMEs are largely unaware. That is, they do not know what they do not know and few are aware of this gap:

> You don't know what it is you don't know – I come across a lot of that, yeah. IT Support

> More and more clients are going on to this VoIP through the Internet so I think they are picking up on this... but that is probably where naivety may come in with a client, maybe not realising how much they can do. . . . Digital Services (IT support)

What made this state of affairs more complex was that although some SMEs do not have some of the skills they need to maximise the potential of SFBB – they think they do:

> I've got all the skills I need to exploit Superfast broadband for what I do, yeah. Web-based Services

> I'm probably not doing everything that you could do but I'm sure I'm making the most of it for what I need... I think so. . . . Tourism and Hospitality

However, in Phase 3 we found far greater awareness of a skills gap than was apparent in Phase 2 with several participants admitting that they need to improve their technical skills:

> I'm sure there's masses of things that I'm not aware of. Architect

The fast-moving pace of the digital economy means that digital skills can quickly become outdated and this contributes to a skills gap:

> The world's changing so fast you daren't say, "Sorted"...you don't know what's coming next, do you? Retail

> I'm realising more and more how many skills we don't have and how many things we don't use that we probably ought to use. Management Consultancy

For many participants, Google was cited as a primary source of looking for information to improve skills and solve technical problems:

> I'd go to Google, that's where I'd look... And very often it's a video of someone explaining it. Fine. Management Consultancy

> Personally I use Google all the time. If there's something, a technical detail I'm not sure about I'll put a very specific search in and 99 times out of 100, within a couple of minutes I've got the answer. Digital Services

However, as one participant pointed out, help was available online but in order to look for it SMEs need to know that they need it, and they need to know where to look:

> You've got online tuition with things, but that's okay if you know how to get there in the first place, a lot of people don't. Digital Services

In Phase 3, we also found evidence of government initiatives to upskill the farming sector who have to use the Internet to record cattle movements as part of a move by DEFRA:

> There was a big move with DEFRA to move stuff on line, which for some farmers is going to be a huge step because ... one of my neighbours, he must be 60 plus, he is not married, he has never been, his animals are his life and he has no interest and yet the need to use the Internet is pushed on him. I think there is going to be some help and there will always be people who will do things for you but when you are being forced to ... well, I think there is a lot of ignorance, I will admit it. Farming and Tourism

In Phase 2, participants often commented that they did not have time to update their skills and there were still some evidence of this in Phase 3 where some claimed lack of time and being too busy running a business as the reasons for not developing skills, unless they were a business requirement:

When you're working flat out it's very difficult to find advice. That's it, time and cost. Financial Services

We probably don't make very good use of it, really. Just uploading, downloading, the speeds are good and that's basically it. We don't really do any marketing or anything, which we could do, we could probably do an awful lot more ... but we don't do at the moment ... we're not savvy. We're a very basic boozer, but then again, we don't have the time, there's only the two of us, we don't have time to do much more than what we do now. You can see a lot of possibilities of it, you know ... but physically finding the time to do it is the hard bit. Tourism and Hospitality

However, in Phase 3, after a longer period of use, we did find evidence that participants are more proactive in seeking to upgrade their skills to maximise the benefits of greater connectivity. It was likely that this was as a result of what we have termed "the virtuous circle of connectivity" – as benefits accrue participants derive more value for their business, become more dependent on those benefits and hence are likely to realise more value and seek out even more. Participants in Phase 3 were also more proactive in seeking out help from others where they could envisage a solution with SFBB but did not know how to implement it. This led several participants to opt for outsourcing to gain access to expertise that could support their aspirations:

The answers are out there and the skills, if you want them, you can hire them. Digital Services

I've said to people before about getting a video, but I don't know, once you've done the video how do you get it onto your website? Because there's all this, is it HTML stuff? And whenever I've tried to add anything to my website with that, it's just gone completely wrong, so I give up and get somebody else to do it. Historical Research

Being cost conscious, several participants mentioned the cost of outsourcing and preferred to use a local network of reciprocal help and support, whether this came via business club contacts or through personal networks:

If you are prepared to pay whatever the cost is of that {outsourcing} is ... Personally I find, certainly living in Cornwall, there's usually a network of people I know, and there's a lot of sort of back-scratching going on, you know? Retail

I've worked a long time in the same sort of area, and I know a lot of people who do a similar sort of thing, and so yes, quite often if there's a problem with hardware, for example, I know a chap who's really good at that so I'll pass it on to him and then something else will come back my way and it all sort of goes around and around like that. IT Support

In Phase 2, we found evidence of a skills gap that was largely unacknow-ledged by SMEs and in Phase 3, for some SMEs, the belief that they know enough to operate effectively was still hampering any upskilling potential and in turn this hinders growth. A major reason for this lack of insight was that participants are not aware of what it was that they do not know. However, in Phase 3 we found more evidence of participants reflecting upon their business practices and the skills necessary to achieve change and we found that SMEs are far more aware of a skills gap than they were in Phase 2. In Phase 3, participants were also more aware that they need to update their skills and were far more proactive in seeking to upskill.

Traditionally, business growth has been dependent on SMEs ability to find, train and retain the best people for the job but that was changing as fibre connectivity opens up opportunities to look for skills globally rather than locally, and on a short-term basis to fit the task in hand. Finding the right staff means finding the right technical skills and in a fast-moving digital economy that can mean looking further afield. SMEs still need to give greater priority to IT training and skills development but where they do not have the required skills themselves, participants are now more proactive in outsourcing to achieve the innovations they envisage and use existing skills networks as well as newly available wider sources of support via the Internet to achieve their goals.

CHAPTER 6

Conclusions, Recommendations and the Future

Abstract In summarising the findings of the Superfast Cornwall project, we can demonstrate clear value for business in the adoption of fibre broadband. However, we can also show that while benefits can be wide ranging, it is not simply the case of providing technology for adoption. Businesses have real skills and knowledge is needed in order to be able to best exploit new technology, and we cannot assume that adoption is smooth and consistent – by its nature, connectivity can be quite diverse depending upon locality whereas businesses often need consistency to maximise benefits.

Keyword Fibre broadband · SMEs · Rural business · Technology adoption

One of the first significant studies of how we might consider the impact of information communications technologies (ICTs) upon organisational performance looking beyond economic measures (Milgrom and Roberts 1990) suggested that there are potentially wider benefits that illustrate the complement between ICT adoption, an organisation's processes and human resource. It was suggested that the impact of the technology does not simply hinge upon the adoption of the technology, but broader investment in aspects of the organisation such as skills development and process change.

© The Author(s) 2017
A. Phippen, H. Lacohée, *The Impact of Fibre Connectivity on SMEs,*
DOI 10.1007/978-3-319-47554-7_6

Subsequent studies have looked at different aspects of impact such as process change as a result of technology adoption and the subsequent impact on efficiency (e.g. Bertschek and Kaiser 2004; Bocquetet al. 2007; Bloom et al. 2012; Koutroumpis 2009; UK Government 2013), while others will focus on the broader aspects such as workforce development and upskilling, in order to best exploit the technological potential (e.g. Caroli and Van Reenen 2001; Bresnahan et al. 2002; Borghans and Ter Weel 2007). Other studies consider all three factors (technology, process change and skills development) as a mix that needs to be successful in order to best exploit the potential of the new technology (e.g. Black and Lynch 2004; Arvanitis and Loukis 2009).

However, the vast majority of these studies take a quantitative dimension, and will generally look inwards at the organisation and its approach to the exploitation of new ICTs. This study has highlighted the importance of also looking outward at the wider business environment and influences, particularly the social structures afforded around small business communities – in understanding these issues in depth, the focus on qualitative inquiry has proved invaluable. Returning to adoption theories such as Diffusion of Innovation (Rogers 2003) and Technology Acceptance Model (Davis 1989) we can see the importance of information resources, the perception of benefit and the role of social structures in encouraging adoption and is certainly reflected in the findings of this work through discourse with business leaders and owners, and allows us to develop theory, *such as the virtuous circle of connectivity*, and make recommendations driven from the voices of those policy is claiming to empower.

There are few studies of small and home-based rural businesses and fewer still that examine the impact of Next Generation Access (NGA) and benefits realisation; most of the studies concerning the introduction of fibre connectivity have focused on fibre access infrastructure. The nature of our sample and the location of the business with whom we researched have meant that this research has conducted very detailed work on this specific area and also looked at a far greater range of factors that impact a lot of studies.

The Internet and digital technology are key drivers for growth for microbusinesses and our research provides compelling evidence of small/ medium enterprises (SMEs) willingness and enthusiasm to embrace the new and exciting opportunities that fibre connectivity affords for business. In earlier phases, we discovered a *virtuous circle of connectivity* through a chain of interdependent benefits that make fibre connectivity invaluable because it enables businesses to avail themselves of digital services such as Cloud technologies that provide benefits that SMEs quickly come to rely on. That reliance builds dependency and reinforces the value of those benefits and as benefits grow new dependencies are forged and a new set of innovations and benefits emerge that are used to even greater effect. This phenomenon maintained in long-term use and small businesses are more dependent on connectivity than ever before.

Our findings reveal that fibre connectivity is playing a pivotal role in increasing SME competiveness and agility, and stimulating productivity, growth and enhanced business innovation. Advances and innovations in ICT in combination with access to a fibre-based broadband network are providing SMEs with a set of powerful tools they are exploiting to work not just faster and more efficiently, but differently. Through long-term use, SMEs have been able to leverage the computational power of Cloud services that enables them to operate as effectively as their larger rivals. In demonstrating the virtuous circle, many more benefits than those discovered in the early stages of adoption have been accrued and demonstrated across a wide range of business activities and across sectors. Simultaneously, electronic trading platforms and Internet banking are providing small businesses with opportunities to serve their markets cost effectively and with the ability to outsource jobs to wider communities of expertise.

Technology has lowered the barriers to operating small businesses effectively and we have seen participants realising and exploiting the benefits of fibre connectivity to grow their business, finding new ways of working, devising new and more efficient processes, exploiting social media for business and increasing networking and collaboration with co-workers in geographically dispersed locations. More than that, digital technologies, and the fibre connectivity that is the vehicle of delivery of those technologies and services, are changing the world of work. This encompasses the way people are employed, how they are employed and when and where they work.

One of the most strongly emerging themes from the analysis of longer-term adoption is that advances in ICT and access to fibre connectivity make running a home-based business a compelling proposition, we have even seen those who were office-based turning to home-based working as a direct result of their new-found efficiencies and productivity gains after 18 months of experience using fibre connectivity.

We are in the midst of a home-based business revolution where the demarcation between work and home is no longer appropriate. What have long been held as the separate spheres of home and work are no longer discrete from each other. Dualistic attitudes that separate home and work as distinct and separate categories have dominated thinking and contributed to the notion that broadband provision should be delivered as either a domestic or a business product. As described in Chap. 5, in ordinary circumstances individuals can easily identify themselves as fitting the dualistic business or a residential profile; superfast broadband (SFBB) provision for work, or for home. However, when the boundaries between work and home are blurred, as is the case of microbusinesses operating from home, the decision is not as straightforward as it might be. Neither a business package nor a consumer package is a good fit for microbusinesses because they need to choose between the conflicting connectivity demands of running a business and satisfying a family's needs for entertainment and cost-effective call bundles. As a result, many microbusinesses are confused about the best option, or whether a suitable option is available at all. To date, there has been little response to the requirements of this large and growing market and this needs to change.

At the start of this text, we stressed that this research was important, not just for understanding the impact of SFBB in Cornwall, but for the general application of fibre optic connectivity in SMEs. We feel we have sufficient replicable findings and come across similar attitudes enough times to be able to be confident that the replication of this exploration among other SME groups, particularly those in rural locations, would achieve similar conclusions. As such, we would present the following key findings from the research:

1. The application of technology is increasingly important to all businesses, regardless of sector and irrespective of their ambitions for growth. In today's fast-paced digital economy, technology has become a part of the everyday business landscape such that fibre connectivity is regarded as a utility; as important as access to water and electricity and something that every business needs in order to survive. In Phase 2, we discovered *the virtuous circle of connectivity*. That reliance builds dependency and reinforces the value of those benefits, and as benefits grow, new dependencies are forged, and a new set of innovations and benefits emerge that are used to even greater effect. This phenomenon maintained with long-term use of SFBB and small businesses are more dependent on connectivity than ever before.

2. The Internet and digital technology are key drivers for growth for microbusinesses and our research provides compelling evidence of SMEs willingness and enthusiasm to embrace the new and exciting opportunities that fibre connectivity affords for business. Advances and innovations in ICT in combination with access to a fibre-based broadband network are providing SMEs with a set of powerful tools, they are exploiting to work not just faster and more efficiently, but differently. Simultaneously, electronic trading platforms and Internet banking are providing small businesses with opportunities to serve their markets cost effectively and with the ability to outsource jobs to wider communities of expertise.

3. When having access to fibre connectivity for 18 months or more, SMEs have been able to leverage the computational power of Cloud services that enables them to operate as effectively as their larger rivals. Through long-term use, many more benefits than those discovered in the early stages of adoption have been accrued and demonstrated across a wide range of business activities and across sectors. The research has seen participants realising and exploiting the benefits of fibre connectivity to grow their business, finding new ways of working, devising new and more efficient processes, exploiting social media for business and increasing networking and collaboration with co-workers in geographically dispersed locations.

4. Digital technologies, and the fibre connectivity that is the vehicle of delivery of those technologies and services, are changing the world of work and this encompasses the way people are employed, how they are employed and when and where they work. The home is fast becoming an important place of business. One of the most strongly emerging themes from Phase 3 is that advances in ICT and access to fibre connectivity make running a home-based business a compelling proposition, we have even seen those who were office-based turning to home-based working as a direct result of their new-found efficiencies and productivity gains after 18 months of experience using fibre connectivity.

5. We heard many complaints concerning reliability and consistency of service; these are complex issues that are interlinked at several levels with problems concerning speed and interruptions to service. Technological constraints impact on the quality of the service that can be delivered to particular premises and in some parts of the region this is more common than in others. Although participants

have complaints about the consistency of service, at present these problems are not impacting on the effective running of business to any significant degree. However, there was some evidence that long-term outages do have a serious impact, especially given businesses growing reliance on their connectivity.

6. When asked about current bandwidth consumption and future needs, participants said current provision had been adequate to accomplish current business needs but this was no longer the case. Many participants report being at the limit of their bandwidth capacity and this is due to the way their use of the Internet has changed; they now depend more heavily on connectivity to operate their businesses and this strongly influences their expectations and aspirations.

7. Business today demands far more upload capacity than was previously required and we saw this in all phases of the research, where participants had started to make use of greater connectivity. However, before they had developed increasing bandwidth demands, the majority did not think symmetry was important. However, if the virtuous circle of connectivity continues at the same pace we have seen, it is possible that while upload demands subside for a time with the increased use of new services, and the subsequent consumption of existing bandwidth, the demand may resurface. We did not get to a point throughout the project where companies had "enough" capacity, they simply used everything they could consume.

8. Bandwidth consumption is set to grow and SMEs are concerned that current broadband provision will not meet their needs in the next 2–5 years. This is a complex issue bound up with the variability in the different levels of service available in different areas across the region – those with the poorest level of service showed the strongest concerns, as did those with the most bandwidth-hungry businesses. There is a strong desire amongst participants to feel that they are future proofed and many are concerned at the increasingly fast pace of domestic consumption that may impact on their ability to run their businesses as effectively as they would like. Again, this is an issue that we first heard in Phase 1 of our research and whilst we have not yet come full circle, SMEs fear that we might. With regard to future proofing participants told us that speed, reliability and consistency of service are still top of their wish list and they will require greater bandwidth provision very shortly in order to maintain their current levels of productivity.

6.1 Key Benefits Realisation

Having experienced SFBB, the value it provides quickly becomes deeply embedded in SMEs daily work practices and processes through benefits realisation and as a result, dependence on connectivity increases. We have found that SFBB has maintained a pivotal role in delivering value through new-found efficiencies, savings, improved business processes and innovations. SFBB is not just an improved way of working; it is a different way of working. SFBB is what makes the web work, it makes the mechanics of delivery transparent and the opportunities it affords are bounded only by the imagination of its users to operate in different ways and develop new innovations. In Phase 3, very few participants felt that the advantages of SFBB were limited to operating more quickly and most were able to describe a much wider range of benefits:

- Rural businesses suffer from remoteness from extended markets but fibre connectivity offers new-found access to global markets that is continuing to promote business growth and enables SMEs to create new revenue streams.
- We found an increased use of Skype conferencing in Phase 2 where participants described how this facility had significantly reduced telephony costs, reduced the need to travel and increased opportunities for collaboration by providing a new, rather than simply an improved way of working. This has endured in Phase 3 and we saw far more widespread use of Skype across a new range of applications for businesses and across different sectors to communicate with clients. Use of Skype continues to have a dramatic impact on how SMEs conduct business and their ability to collaborate, changing not only what can be achieved but also the way it is achieved.
- We found increasing evidence of participants accessing a broader customer base as a result of fibre connectivity in Phase 3. Greater connectivity is providing SMEs with greater confidence, enabling them to broaden their customer base within the UK and further afield and this is supporting business growth in the region.
- In facilitating the use of Cloud services, SFBB offers SMEs the opportunity to revolutionise the way they work and compete far more effectively with their larger rivals. Cloud services offer SMEs the opportunity to reduce their IT expenditure and this provides flexibility and frees up funds that can be directed towards other aspects of the

business. The ease, convenience and cost savings Cloud services provide are set to play an increasingly important role in the evolution of
SME IT operations. In Phase 3, after longer experience of using
SFBB, increased use of Cloud services is proving transformative for
business and emerging as a major disruptive force.

- Fibre connectivity is enabling SMEs to remain located in Cornwall,
  protecting existing jobs and is providing the infrastructure that
  helps overcome the region's peripheral location. There is evidence
  of job creation but employment patterns are changing with
  increased collaboration on short-term contracts both locally and
  farther afield. Many start-ups are operating from home and businesses are downsizing due to increased efficiencies with SFBB and
  swapping office-based working for home-based working.

- Business growth is vital in today's financial climate and SMEs said their
  ability to operate at all, particularly in Cornwall, is wholly dependent on
  greater and more efficient connectivity that enables them to exploit
  technological advances. SFBB is supporting businesses in the region
  with strong growth ambitions and encouraging diversification and new
  opportunities for growth that would not otherwise be possible.

- Today's SMEs inhabit a world that is undergoing a culture of change
  and they need to develop the right skills to operate effectively. Using
  social media in a business context is one such example and in Phase 3 we
  saw an increase in using social media across a far more diverse range of
  activities than we had seen in Phase 2. Only a minority did not use any
  form of social media at all for business and the most often cited reason
  was lack of time. To some extent whether or not SMEs use social media
  and the value that they derive is sector dependent, but most feel that it is
  now a business tool that cannot be ignored and one that can bring
  enormous benefits. The need to use social media regularly to maintain
  relationships with customers was a deterrent to some in terms of the
  amount of time they felt would be needed to be dedicated to keeping up
  that activity but others found it a vital and invaluable tool.

- In Phase 2, participants were enthusiastic about the competitive edge
  SFBB has delivered over the rest of the country but as roll-out has
  increased over Phase 3, this enthusiasm has waned. However, without fibre connectivity businesses in the region could not remain
  competitive and many would not be able to operate at all. It is
  inevitable that the competitive advantage of being amongst the first
  to have access to fibre will wane with increased roll-out across the

UK, but it is still helping to create a level playing field for a region that suffers the disadvantages of a peripheral location and poor road, rail and air infrastructure.

6.2   MAXIMISING BENEFITS

In Phase 2, we found evidence of a skills gap that is largely unacknowledged by SMEs and in Phase 3, for some SMEs, the belief that they know enough to operate effectively is still hampering any upskilling potential and in turn this hinders growth. A major reason for this lack of insight is that participants are not aware of what it is that they do not know. However, in Phase 3 we found more evidence of participants reflecting upon their business practices and the skills necessary to achieve change and we found that SMEs are far more aware of a skills gap than they were in Phase 2. In Phase 3, participants were also more aware that they need to update their skills and were far more proactive in seeking to upskill. Where they do not have the required skills themselves, they are also more proactive in outsourcing to achieve the innovations they envisage and use existing skills networks as well as newly available wider sources of support via the Internet to achieve this. Appropriate and adequate IT equipment is an important strategic asset that is necessary to make the most of fibre connectivity. We found less evidence of participants upgrading their IT equipment in Phase 3 than we saw in Phase 2 but this is possibly because in Phase 2 participants described upgrading when they initially signed up for SFBB. It is likely that the increase in use of Cloud services we have observed in Phase 3 also plays a role here in that this helps to reduce capital spend. There is still some evidence of SMEs using old and outdated IT equipment and software and we found there is reluctance amongst some SMEs to upgrade until they have to, that is, when equipment breaks down or cannot be repaired.

6.3   RECOMMENDATIONS

Based upon the findings of our research we offer the following key recommendations for those wishing to deploy and encourage the adoption of SFBB services to SMEs:

- Dualistic thinking that separates work and home as distinct categories for broadband provision is outdated and inappropriate. Advances in ICT and access to fibre connectivity have given rise to a large market of home-based microbusinesses of growing economic significance that have been largely ignored by Internet Service Providers (ISPs). To meet this trend and support government economic strategy it is necessary for ISPs to respond with an appropriate service offering. There is a clear gap in the market for a tailored package to fit the needs of those operating a business from home that takes account of business needs for fast and reliable connectivity and fast fault resolution as well as domestic requirements for entertainment and call bundles. Given the diverse requirements of microbusiness across various sectors there is unlikely to be a "one size fits all" solution and a suite of add-ons from which microbusiness can choose the most effective combination for their particular needs is likely to be the most appropriate option.

- There is a strong requirement for fibre connectivity to be standardised. Connectivity is sold to customers on the basis of advertised "up to" broadband speeds, but due to technological constraints few participants were able to achieve these speeds and feel aggrieved as a result. This is contributing to the reported customer dissatisfaction with broadband speed (see Sec. 6.3) and is likely to be contributing to the number of reported fibre "faults". Instead, connectivity should be provided on the basis of delivering a guaranteed minimum speed rather than an aspirational "up to" speed.
- Demands on bandwidth are growing as businesses become more dependent on connectivity and domestic users consume bandwidth-hungry entertainment services. Added to this there is a growing need for the capacity to connect ever increasing numbers of people and devices. Businesses are worried that domestic consumption may impact on their ability to run their businesses effectively and service providers need to be prepared to meet demand with increased bandwidth capacity and faster services, better upload speeds and more widespread provision of Fibre to the Premise (FTTP).
- The roll-out of fibre services is crucial, more SMEs need access to a powerful Internet connection to support their business growth and it is time to fill the gaps in fibre connectivity provision. Availability of fibre broadband is influencing where people choose to live and whether or not they are able to conduct a business. In turn, lack of access to fibre connectivity is influencing property prices and hindering business growth. It is also contributing to the move from office-based working where connectivity is not available, to home-based working where it is, the reverse of this is also likely to be true but the present study cannot

report any evidence. There is a strong need to fill the gaps in provision and make access to fibre broadband inclusive with roll-out to hard to reach isolated rural locations and town centres to hasten growth opportunities for business and maximise exploitation of fibre connectivity.

- Microbusinesses operating from home have long been thought of and referred to as "invisible businesses" because (erroneously) they were not thought to make a significant contribution to the economy. As a result, until recently, they have been largely ignored by government, policymakers and service providers alike as of little consequence. As a result, legislation and regulation have been designed for a world in which the workplace and the home are separate. The same is true of ISPs who cater either for a business or a domestic market and both are examples of dualistic thinking characterised by a discrete separation of home and work. Government is now responding to this important trend with a number of initiatives to support home-based businesses and new measures have been announced that will create greater freedom to start a business from home, similarly ISPs also need to respond. However, because this large and growing market has been ignored, little is known or understood about home-based businesses operating in a fast-paced digital world and therefore further research is called for.

Overall, a key finding of this research is that the adoption of SFBB follows the routes proposed by adoption theories. It is not simply a case of providing the technology and assuming adoption will happen. Businesses need to understand key operation and strategic benefits to the technology, and there need to be routes for them to learn about them through peer networks, effective and accurate communication channels and trusted change agents. In the event of a dearth of information, the vacuum will be filled by assumption and conjecture, which can be extremely counterproductive to successful adoption.

In addition, policymakers and technology providers need to acknowledge the learning curve with the use of new technology, and understand that the benefits are incremental – the more a technology is used and mainstreamed into the business, the more the business will discover can be done with it. A focus on short-term benefits and simple geographical distribution, which may be useful indicators of a policy success, are far less effective at achieving business regeneration than long-term study and understanding the breadth of issues that arise.

However, overall, this research has shown that technologies can have lasting, long-term impact upon business development and growth, as long as support and information is available and embracing other facets of technology adoption, such as communication channels and social structures, are considered as important as the technology itself.

REFERENCES

Arvanitis, S., & Loukis, E. N. (2009). Information and communication technologies, human capital, workplace organization and labour productivity: A comparative study related on firm-level data for Greece and Switzerland. *Information Economics and Policy, 21*(1), 43–61.

Bertschek, I., & Kaiser, U. (2004). Productivity effects of organizational change: Microeconometric evidence. *Management Science, 50*(3), 394–404.

Black, S. E., & Lynch, L. M. (2004). What's driving the new economy? The benefits of workplace innovation. *The Economic Journal, 114*(493), F97–F116.

Bloom, N., Sadun, R., & Van Reenen, J. (2012). Americans do I.T. better: US multinationals and the productivity miracle. *American Economic Review, 102,* 167–201.

Bocquet, R., Brossard, O., & Sabatier, M. (2007). Complementarities in organizational design and the diffusion of information technologies: An empirical analysis. *Research Policy, 36,* 367–386.

Borghans, L., & Ter Weel, B. (2007). The diffusion of computers and the distribution of wages. *European Economic Review, 51*(3), 715–748.

Bresnahan, T. F., Brynjolfsson, E., & Hitt, L. M. (2002). Information technology, workplace organization and the demand for skilled labor: Firm-level evidence. *The Quarterly Journal of Economics, 117,* 339–376.

Caroli, E., & Van Reenen, J. (2001). Skill-biased organizational change? Evidence from a panel of British and French establishments. *The Quarterly Journal of Economics, 116*(4), 1449–1492.

Davis, F. D. (1989). Perceived usefulness, perceived ease of use, and user acceptance of information technology. *MIS Quarterly, 13*(3), 319–340.

Koutroumpis, P. (2009). The economic impact of broadband on growth: A simultaneous approach. *Telecommunications Policy, 33,* 471–485.

Milgrom, P., & Roberts, J. (1990). Bargaining costs, influence costs, and the organization of economic activity. In J. Alt & K. Shepsle (Eds..), *Perspectives on positive political economy.* Cambridge: Cambridge University Press.

Rogers, E. (2003). *The diffusion of innovations* (5th ed.). New York: The Free Press.

UK Government. (2013). UK broadband impact study: Literature review. https://www.gov.uk/government/publications/uk-broadband-impact-study [Accessed July 2016].

Appendix – Discussion Guides for Each Project Phase

Phase 1

Superfast Cornwall

SME Focus Group Moderator Guide

Introduction

Welcome, introductions (Andy, Hazel, any observers):

- Consent, recording, use of data;
- Confidentiality;
- Right to withdraw;
- Incentive arrangements;
- Fire exits;
- Purpose of groups (very brief description of Superfast Cornwall project, our need to understand customer needs and expectations);
- What we will do with the data;
- One person one voice.

Round table, participants to introduce selves: name, what your company does, your role and responsibilities.

© The Author(s) 2017
A. Phippen, H. Lacohée, *The Impact of Fibre Connectivity on SMEs*,
DOI 10.1007/978-3-319-47554-7

Initial response to, awareness and understanding of SFBB

So what is SFBB? What do you know about it?

How did you find out about it/where do you look for information about SFBB?

How much is it? Is that what you expected? Is that good value?

Do you know enough about it to decide whether or not you'd want it?

Do you think it will live up to your expectations?

Who's already decided they want it, don't want it, not sure (show of hands)?

(Explore in depth yes – how soon? no and not sure according to responses – what impacts on those decisions?)

Current ISP, anybody planning to change as a result of SFBB availability?

Current experience and expectations

What are the key applications and current bandwidth absorbers?

What kind of issues/problems do you have currently? Uploading/downloading

(*Prompt: Are there things that you would like to do but can't because you don't have enough bandwidth?*)

How does that impact your business?

How important is that to you?

How do you solve those problems currently?

Expectations

When first generation BB was first introduced to Cornwall did that make a difference to your business?

How, in what way?

How important is that to you?

Do you think moving to SFBB will make the same sort of impact as moving from dial up to BB or is it different?

How, in what way?

How important is that to you?

Prompts:

What will SFBB enable you to do?

a) Faster;
b) More efficiently
c) Could not do before?
d) Do you think SFBB will help you develop new products and services?
e) Will it change the way you do things now, for example, email and Facebook did with first generation broadband? What kind of changes?*
f) Will SFBB enable you to create more jobs?*
g) Will SFBB impact on the way you work?
   Prompt: How? In what way? What would change/stay the same? How important are those factors to you?
h) Will it enable you to work more flexibly? For example, could some of your staff work from home/do you see yourself recruiting flexible workers? Will it create more scope for flexible working for you?*
i) Will SFBB help you combat the current economic conditions? How, in what way?*

What, specifically, could SFBB could do for *your* business? (Round table)

Prompt: What impact would it have, what are the advantages? (*prompt: will it make you more competitive? Able to upload more as well as download?*)

Are those reasons the major drivers for wanting SFBB, is there anything else?

Will it impact on home/domestic use, in what way?

Will it impact on other aspects of life – for example, the amount of travelling you have to do? Time with family, etc.?

What else might it impact on?

Concerns/issues

Do you have any concerns about whether you will need different skill sets to take advantage of SFBB?

Would you welcome any training around the uses of SFBB, for example, videoconferencing, Cloud computing?

Do you have any concerns about whether you will need to change/upgrade your equipment?

Do have any concerns about SFBB or web-based activities more generally? For example, privacy, security concerns?
What would stand in the way of you getting SFBB?

Future aspirations

What kind of services could SFBB offer that would appeal to you?
How do you see your business in 5 years' time and how important is SFBB to achieving that?
Is there anything that you don't think SFBB can do that you wish it could?
What haven't we talked about that you wish we'd covered?
Has anyone changed their mind about wanting/not wanting/still unsure of SFBB?

Wrap up

Thank you all for coming and taking part, it is been really useful for us, if anyone has any questions

PHASE 2

Introduction

Welcome, introductions, consent, recording, use of data:

- Confidentiality;
- Right to withdraw;
- Incentive arrangements;
- Fire exits;
- Purpose of groups (very brief description of Superfast Cornwall project, our need to understand customer needs, expectations and experience);
- What we will do with the data;
- One rule: one person one voice.

Round table, participants to introduce selves: name, what your company does, your role/responsibilities.

Expectations

1. What made you decide to upgrade to SFBB?
2. Do you know what kind of speeds you are getting now with SFBB compared with previous BB provision?
3. Is your experience of SFBB what you expected? Is it better/worse/same? How does it compare with the move from dial up to BB?
4. Has anyone opted for the faster (80/20 Mb) FTTC product?
   Prompts: What influenced that decision?
   Experience of the product/value to business
   How does it compare with previous speeds?
5. Is SFBB good value for money?
6. Do you intend to keep SFBB/upgrade?
7. Are you with the same ISP now as you were for BB? (Quick round up of who they are with) Is anyone thinking of changing? Why?

Business Impact

1. What impact has SFBB had on your business and how important is that to you?
   Prompts: Working faster/more efficiently/effectively
   Increased productivity
   Develop new products/services *(identify potential case studies)*
   Work/life balance
   Has it changed how/when you work? How/in what way?
   What sort of problems has it helped you to overcome?
2. Has SFBB enabled you to:
   Make use of different applications/services, for example, Cloud, videoconferencing?
   Take advantage of improved upload and download speeds?
   Take on more employees/expand business – was this partly/wholly due to SFBB?
   Might you take on more staff in the course of the next 2 years as a result of SFBB;

Work with a wider range of people either as employees – or extending your customer base;
Use more flexible working practices;
Connect more people/devices;
Change working patterns/practices/do things you couldn't do or were difficult to do before;
Create new business/more jobs;
Build better collaborative networks;
Achieve tasks in house that were previously outsourced;
Combat current economic conditions/increase competitiveness;
Make more/better use of social networking sites for business;
Accomplish more online, for example, reduce the need to travel/use of couriers to send large files, etc.
Ask how important each of the issues above is to participants and in what way it has improved business.

3. Do you think SFBB will enable you to decrease your carbon footprint? How important is this to you? Introduce carbon calculator tool, provide handouts

4. Has SFBB enabled you to do things that you hadn't previously thought of?
   Prompts: Get examples, for example, new products/services or ways of doing things.
   What difference does that make to your business?

5. Has SFBB availability impacted your ability to stay located in Cornwall?

6. Whether or not you are now doing things differently, what is the most important difference SFBB has made to your business and why?

Maximising SFBB benefits

1. Do you feel you know enough about SFBB capability to take full advantage for your business?

2. Is there anything that could improve your SFBB experience?

3. Do you need different/additional skills to make the most of SFBB?
   Prompt: What kind of skills, where/how will you acquire them?

4. Have you changed/upgraded IT kit as a result of getting SFBB? Do you think you need to/will in the future?

5. Do you have any security or privacy issues with SFBB over and above any issues you might have had before with BB? For example, using new services
   Prompt: Examples/what are you doing about it?
6. Are you experiencing or do you anticipate any problems with SFBB?

Future aspirations

1. What kind of new services could SFBB offer that would appeal to you?
2. How do you see your business in 5 years time and how important is SFBB to achieving that?
3. Is there anything that you don't think SFBB can do that you wish it could?
4. Do you think SFBB provision in Cornwall will attract inward investment? What difference could that make to the region?

Wrap up

Is there anything we haven't talked about that you wish we'd covered?

Thank you all for coming and taking part, it's been really useful for us, don't forget to collect incentives, if anyone has any questions, etc.

PHASE 3

Introduction

Welcome, introductions, consent, recording, use of data:

- Confidentiality;
- Right to withdraw;
- Incentive arrangements;
- Fire exits;
- Purpose of groups (our need to better understand customer needs, expectations and experience);
- What we will do with the data;
- One rule: one person one voice;

Round table, participants to introduce selves: name, what your company does, your role/responsibilities.

Expectations

1. Has SFBB met with your expectations now that you've been using it for 18 months plus?
   Prompts: is it better, worse, same?
2. Is it good value for money? Are there any associated costs you hadn't considered?
3. Do you know what kind of speeds you are getting now with SFBB compared with previous BB provision?
4. Is it fast enough to accomplish everything you want to do now?
   Prompt: Are participants still looking for a symmetrical service?
5. What applications etc. are your biggest bandwidth consumers?
6. Will it be fast enough to accommodate your plans for the future?
7. Has anyone opted for/would like FTTP? (*show of hands*)
   Prompts: What influences that decision?
   Experience of the product/value to business
   How does it compare with previous speeds?
8. Are you with the same ISP now as you were for BB? (Quick round up of who they are with) Is anyone thinking of changing? Why?
9. Business or consumer product?
   What influences that choice?
   Is it good enough for what you want?
   What do you want from a business product?

Innovation: What has changed: Business Impact/Business practice changes

1. What is the most important impact SFBB has had on your business and how important is that to you?
   Prompts: Working faster/more efficiently/effectively
   Increased productivity, time/money;
   Reduced or increased travel;
   Business growth – develop new products/services (identify potential case studies);
   Work/life balance;

Has it changed how/when you work? How/in what way?
What sort of problems has it helped you to overcome?
Work with a wider range of people either as employees – or
*   extending your customer base/better collaboration;*
Use more flexible working practices;
Use of applications;
Differences in collaboration patterns, changes in access to
*   markets (international market expansion);*
Remote data storage;
Sending large files;
Video/web conferencing/Skype;
Remote access/working from home;
Using social media;
Connecting multiple devices;

2. Job creation/retention
   Has SFBB enabled you to create more jobs, retain the jobs you have, lose any jobs?
   Do you have plans to create/retain/lose jobs?
   Might you take on more staff in the course of the next 2–5 years as a result of SFBB?
3. Has SFBB enabled you to diversify/create a new business/grow your business?
4. Has SFBB enabled you to use new software platforms?
   Make use of different applications/services, for example, Cloud, videoconferencing?
   Take advantage of improved upload and download speeds?
   Connect more people/devices;
   Change working patterns/practices/do things you couldn't do or were difficult to do before;
   Build better collaborative networks;
   Achieve tasks in house that were previously outsourced;
   Combat current economic conditions/increase competitiveness;
   Make more/better use of social networking sites for business.
   Accomplish more online, for example, reduce the need to travel/use of couriers to send large files, etc.
   Ask how important each of the issues above is to participants and in what way it has improved business.
5. What are you using it for now that you didn't use before?

6. What has SFBB enabled you to do that you hadn't previously thought of?
   Prompts: Get examples, for example, new products/services or ways of doing things.
   What difference does that make to your business?
7. What is consuming the most bandwidth in your current use? Is that likely to change?
8. Has SFBB availability impacted your ability to stay located in Cornwall?
   Prompts: Does it influence your choice of location for your business?
   Has it created a level playing field?

Maximising SFBB benefits

1. Do you feel you have adequate IT skills to take full advantage of SFBB for your business? Has your skill set changed as a result of having SFBB?
2. Do you need different/additional skills to make the most of SFBB?
   Prompt: What kind of skills, where/how will you acquire them?
   Where do you go to for advice?
3. Have you changed/upgraded IT kit as a result of getting SFBB? Do you think you need to/will in the future?
4. Is there anything that could improve your SFBB experience?

Problems/frustrations

1. Are you experiencing or do you anticipate any problems with SFBB?
   Prompt: is it fast enough? Will it be fast enough for your future bandwidth requirements?
2. Do you have any fears or frustrations with SFBB?
   Prompts: include skills/lack of, operational issues, etc., need for an appropriately tailored micro business package, etc.)
   What are you able/would like to see done about that?
3. Do you have any security or privacy issues with SFBB over and above any issues you might have had before with BB? For example, using new services like Cloud.
   Prompt: Examples/what are you doing about it?
4. Do you think SFBB has had any impact on your carbon footprint? How important is this to you? *Provide handouts to participants with at end*

Future aspirations

1. How do you see your business in 5 years time and how important is SFBB to achieving that? What plans do you have for the future that depend on SFBB capability?
2. What kind of new services could SFBB offer that would appeal to you?
3. Is there anything that you don't think SFBB can do that you wish it could?
4. Do you think SFBB provision in Cornwall will attract inward investment?
   What difference could that make to the region?
5. What would you say to someone in your business who hasn't yet taken up SFBB to persuade them to change?

Wrap up

Is there anything we haven't talked about that you wish we'd covered?

Thank you all for coming and taking part, it's been really useful for us, don't forget to collect incentives, if anyone has any questions, etc.

Index

© The Author(s) 2017
A. Phippen, H. Lacohée, *The Impact of Fibre Connectivity on SMEs,*
DOI 10.1007/978-3-319-47554-7

Printed in the United States
By Bookmasters